THE ENCYCLOPAEDIA OF PATTERNS AND MOTIFS

THE ENCYCLOPAEDIA OF PATTERNS AND MOTIFS

A COLLECTION OF 5000 DESIGNS FROM CULTURES AROUND THE WORLD

Dorothy Bosomworth

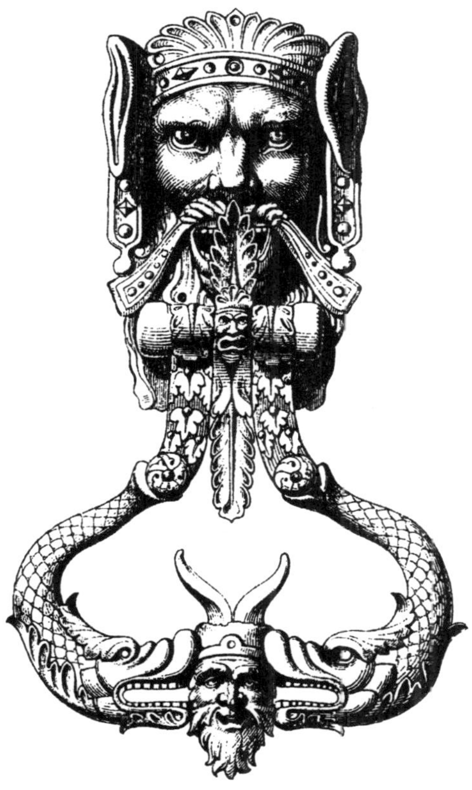

S
STUDIO

Acknowledgements

The author, Dorothy Bosomworth,

would like to thank the following for their assistance and co-operation:

Charlotte Deane, for picture research; Mei Lim, book designer;

Alison Moss, editor, and her colleagues at Studio.

She also wishes to thank Vanessa Fletcher, Lianne Jarrett, Julia Hanson,

Jim and Elizabeth Laidlaw, Jo Newson, Marie O'Flaherty, Keith Sugden,

Isobel Watson and the staff of the British Library, the London Library

and the National Art Library.

First published in 1995 by Studio
an imprint of Random House UK Ltd
20 Vauxhall Bridge Road, London SW1V 2SA

Reprinted 1997, 1998

Picture research by Charlotte Deane
Designed by Mei Lim

ISBN 1 85891 221 0

Printed and bound in Singapore.

CONTENTS

INTRODUCTION

This inspirational encyclopaedia provides a rich visual anthology of decorative patterns and motifs, while at the same time forming a visual primer, offering a basis for synthesis and comparison. Organized according to continents, five chapters cover Europe, Asia and Africa, the Americas and Australasia (including Oceania).

The European chapter is arranged chronologically, from the classical civilizations of ancient Crete and Greece, Rome and Etruria to the end of the nineteenth century. The other chapters are organized geographically: selections from the Americas and Africa move from north to south, while Asia and Australasia range from west to east.

The systematic study of pattern first gained popular momentum in the nineteenth century as a result of several factors: the development of art and design education, the establishment of art history as an academic discipline, the foundation and growth of the major national museums and galleries, and the sequence of nineteenth-century international exhibitions of art and industry.

In the Western hemisphere, national museums and learned academic societies supported ambitious and competitive programmes of travel and research, collecting and publication, prompting the publication of a number of popular encyclopaedias of ornament. However, their authors were limited in their world view, paying scant attention to native cultures, and scarcely heeding their intrinsic dignity. This encyclopaedia sets out to redress that balance.

Looking at the rich diversity of imagery contained in this book, it is possible to identify common characteristics between the decorative patterns and motifs of different cultures. One is consequently tempted to speculate further on possible inter-continental links between the art forms of one culture and another. Fascinating as these speculations are, they fall beyond the scope of this book.

The range of objects illustrated is extremely broad. Each page contains an exciting array of carefully selected images showing architectural details, sculpture, painting, mosaics, tiles; domestic and ecclesiastical artefacts: glass, ceramics, inscriptions, manuscripts, metalwork, furniture, textiles, costume, jewellery; items concerned with tribal ceremonies and rituals: pipes, masks, weapons, symbolic images and totems.

Many of these items have been made within established traditions, for specific purposes. Decoration is sometimes compressed within tightly confined areas. Bear in mind therefore that the creative autonomy of the respective architect, artist, craftsman or designer may have been extremely limited. Yet it is precisely how quality of design and freedom of aesthetic expression is achieved despite these constraints that makes these artefacts so fascinating.

In addition to considering cultural evolution and dissemination, this eclectic collection of images raises a number of other issues: the relationships between design and production, material, technique and decoration, training, patronage and purpose. With the advent of the Industrial Revolution from the mid eighteenth century, and the nineteenth-century processes of European colonial expansion and emigration, metal tools were disseminated worldwide. Even remote communities, such as those in the Polynesian islands of the South Pacific Ocean, were able to use knives for wood carving, which in turn affected the quality and character of their work.

Historians of European decorative art are accustomed to think of artistic training as a pattern of studio apprenticeship by gifted individuals, and professional practice within the guild system. Among cultures with strong religious traditions, the monastic system historically provides a context in which artistic training and practice can flourish. For native non-industrialized cultures, such as the North West Coastal Indians of North America, the Maoris of New Zealand or the Australian Aborigines, the situation was different.

There, pattern-making as part of craft activity was practised by anyone in the community, although certain individuals might be especially talented. Decorative imagery on clothing and artefacts was perceived as a means of communication, and could have ritual celebratory significance, as well as indicating tribal status. Art in this context became an expression of common purpose, as well as a source of employment. Parallels exist within contemporary Western culture, in communal preparation for carnivals, for example.

One other major factor must be taken into consideration: purpose. Within western cultures, pieces could be commissioned by the Crown, the aristocracy, the state, private clients, or made speculatively for sale. Within an ethnic context, pieces might be made for ritual religious purposes, to denote tribal status, or for barter. In some cases, the concept of trade as we know it in the West did not exist: artefacts therefore did not have an external economic value.

Whilst it is important to understand this context historically, on a worldwide basis, the dangers which exist now with world tourism are also significant. There may be a threat to the instrinsic individual quality and purpose of artefacts originally made within a much more specific and confined frame of reference.

EUROPE

European decorative patterns and motifs were subject to a number of important influences: the classical tradition of ancient Greece and Rome; the abstract curvilinear forms of the Celts – the first of the barbarian invasions – ultimately traceable to sources in central Asia; Islamic art.

Classical architecture is symmetrical and carefully proportioned, based on a post and lintel system derived from wooden construction, using stone or marble for its major buildings. Low relief sculptural ornament was frequently confined to the upper levels of a building: to capitals on columns, and to the various components of an entablature or lintel. Colour was originally carefully applied; statues of gods or goddesses were gilded; friezes were highly coloured.

The three orders of Greek architecture – Doric, Ionic and Corinthian – are characterized by the types of capitals which they use. Each order contains its own system of proportion. Characteristic types of ornament used include spiral scrolls, egg-and-dart mouldings, fret and Greek key borders, and the acanthus leaf. Greek vases show considerable mastery of form and figural decoration, the latter often within confined spaces. Roman and Etruscan mosaic pavements display a remarkable combination of different complex geometric patterns within a harmonious whole.

In 330 AD Constantine was crowned Roman Emperor. His adoption of Christianity as the official imperial religion marks the start of the Byzantine Empire, which lasted until 1453 AD. The fall of Rome to the Visigoths in 410 AD heralded the beginning of the 'Dark Ages' in Europe, as a series of tribal invasions from eastern Europe swept westwards. These two events signal a divide in cultural development, and its consequent decorative effects.

Byzantine art represents a synthesis of classical and oriental influences. Using mosaics, wall paintings and sculpture as public art forms, it developed an elaborate language of Christian symbolic and pictorial imagery that was used extensively in its chapels and basilicas. Through gifts and diplomatic missions, Byzantine woven silk fabrics found their way into European collections, as did superb illuminated manuscripts with elaborate jewel-embossed metal covers.

The Visigoths were part of a wave of invading tribes from eastern Europe which included Celts, Vandals and Huns, Angles, Saxons and Vikings. These tribes introduced new styles into European decorative pattern, including complex semi-abstract animal and serpent interlace patterns, used widely in metalwork and jewellery. The new forms also appeared later in early Christian illuminated manuscripts and on incised stone slabs and crosses, produced at monasteries in Ireland and the north of England in the seventh and eighth centuries.

On the continent, the Carolingian empire, under the reign of Charlemagne (743 – 814) witnessed a revival of interest in classical art and culture, seen in new metalwork, jewellery, furniture, illuminated manuscripts and architecture.

Christianity was a major influence on European medieval art and architecture. The growth of monasticism throughout Europe led to a vigorous programme of building abbeys and priories, and provided a stable environment within which there was a ready demand for religious art and crafts. Within Romanesque architecture from the tenth to the early twelfth centuries, the decorative emphasis was on sculpture and wall paintings. Gothic architecture, dominant between the eleventh and fifteenth centuries, continued to use sculpture extensively, but was also noted for its extensive use of stained glass.

The Renaissance – a rebirth and creative reinterpretation of the Roman Classical Tradition – began in Florence, Italy, in the first quarter of the fifteenth century and from there spread to Milan, Venice and throughout Northern Italy to reach Rome by the end of the century. Renaissance ornament brought to the classical tradition a sense of elegance and grace. Rivalry between different Italian states, along with the omnipresent influence of the Church, created a political and religious milieu in which art and design flourished, thanks to generous patronage.

The concept of 'design' came into vogue during the Renaissance. The word is derived from the Italian *disegno*, meaning a preparatory drawing to serve as a model. By about 1500, goldsmiths, painters and engravers dominated design. By 1530, mural painters, sculptors and architects became involved. Working on major commissions for great courts, they assembled and trained teams of specialist designers and craftsmen. This set the trend for the processes of royal and aristocratic patronage and training which prevailed throughout Europe from the sixteenth century onwards.

The influence of the Renaissance spread into France during the last quarter of the fifteenth century. Due to the prevalence of the gothic style, at first the new influence was confined to decorative details, but by the reign of the King François I (1494 – 1547), it had gained wider sway.

The Renaissance was absorbed into Germany from France, but for a number of reasons, it did not develop in a homogenous way. The strength of the Gothic idiom, Protestantism, the fragmented governmental structure of Germany and the Thirty Years' War all had an effect. Pattern books of designs by Hans Burkmair and Hans Holbein demonstrating the new style circulated widely, but it was not until Italian artists worked directly in Germany that the new style was properly absorbed and understood.

Renaissance influences moved into Spain from France and Italy towards the end of the fifteenth century. At first, they were absorbed into the Plateresque or goldsmith's style, characterized by a lavish use of decorative motifs unrelated to the structure of the building. Later, a purer, Graeco-Roman inspired style came into being in architecture.

The Renaissance was followed in the seventeenth and eighteenth centuries by the Baroque style, more pronounced in southern Europe than elsewhere. Architecture was united with sculpture and painting, to create visual and spatial effects which relied on illusionism, a play of light and colour, and movement for their dramatic impact. In France, the royal palace at Versailles, remodelled for Louis XIV, typified the new style.

During the eighteenth century, two different cultural movements - rococo and neo-classicism - affected the appearance of decorative patterns and motifs. The rococo movement (from the French *rocaille,* meaning shell) was associated with fantasy and romanticism: sinuous curves, delicate scrollwork and an abundance of ornament graced furniture, metalwork, textiles, porcelain and engraved illustrations.

Neo-classicism marked a return to ancient Greek and Roman ornamentation for inspiration. Architects, artists and designers such as Robert Adam travelled to study original sources before reinterpreting these for their clients. Starting in the 1740s, the excavation of Herculaneum and Pompeii, two important Roman cities, created keen public interest in the delicate grace of Pompeian wall paintings and artefacts.

The French Revolution and the subsequent rise to imperial power of Napoleon further endorsed this association between contemporary taste and classical Rome. In the early nineteenth century, his lavish patronage promoted luxurious craftsmanship of the highest quality. At a more popular level, classicism influenced furniture and interior design throughout Europe during the 1820s to 1840s.

The classical revival was challenged by a number of architects and designers, who instead championed the Gothic style. For some, the whole debate had important ideological significance concerned with Roman Catholicism versus Protestantism. For others, this choice was one aspect of the stylistic pluralism which dominated mid nineteenth-century architecture and design.

It was not until the 1870s that the Aesthetic Movement, with its interests in nature and in the art of Japan, offered an escape from the straitjacket of historicism. By the 1890s, the impetus of an imminent new century prompted the rise of Art Nouveau, an international movement within architecture, art and design. Its attenuated forms, sinuous grace and semi-abstract patterns were widely published. The new look was adopted *en masse* for the Paris International Exhibition of 1900.

ASIA

Asia's rich variety of cultures have produced a vast wealth of imagery that is of perennial fascination to the Western world.

The chapter devoted to Asia begins with a selection of images from Assyria, the ancient empire centred on the banks of the Tigris and Euphrates rivers, in present-day Iraq. Many of its major buildings were excavated in the nineteenth century, revealing architectural skill and decorative designs of remarkable quality and sophistication. The images are frequently strong and dramatic, as in the friezes from the palace at Nimrud that featured lions and winged bulls, typically seen in profile, now in the British Museum.

Persian design is noted for the grace and fluidity with which surface pattern is handled, whether in designs using floral motifs, or in calligraphic and geometric patterns. Its particular ability to combine patterns of different scales and rhythms effectively through its textiles and its ceramics is of continuing interest to Western designers.

Much decorative imagery in Indian architecture appears in the context of religious buildings, including shrines and temples. The most famous example is undoubtedly the Taj Mahal, with its exquisite tile inlays. Throughout India, the buildings of the various religious sects use decorative designs for pierced openwork screens, sculpture and surface ornament. Whatever the caste in question, religious architectural ornament is frequently distinguished by its rhythmic flow and intricate use of pattern. Even in smaller items, such as textiles or inlaid enamels, for example, the ability to handle the rhythmic flow of line in a condensed space is strongly apparent.

Specific religious traditions in different parts of Asia encourage the practice of particular crafts. So, in Tibet for instance, there are outstanding examples of cast bronze, used both for statues of Buddhist deities and other devotional artefacts, such as bells.

The rhythmic flow of floral and foliate pattern is also characteristic of Chinese blue and white ceramics, from which a number of designs are published. Collected in the West since the eighteenth century, Chinese blue and white ceramics retain an enduring freshness of appeal.

Japan remained closed to the West from the seventeenth century to the mid nineteenth century. Since that time, its art forms have been avidly studied and collected in the West. Like the Chinese, the Japanese have outstanding standards of craftsmanship in ceramics, textiles, metalwork, and in calligraphic painting, among other art forms. Inlaid metal sword mounts and noblemen's badges illustrated in this section demonstrate the skill and artistry of Japanese craftsmen in achieving inventive creativity within highly restricted areas. Images of fish and plants reveal the abilities of Japanese artists in conveying grace within natural illustration.

In the island cultures of South East Asia the native peoples use local woods and palm leaves to fashion a range of products. Included for illustration in this section is a typical selection from Sumatra. Examples show an intricate sense of dense decorative pattern that uses both arabesque and interlace designs for metalwork and for lidded boxes and jewellery.

AFRICA

This chapter is divided into three sections, dealing with ancient Egypt, the art of Islam, and sub-equatorial native art. It is extremely difficult to make any generalizations about African art, because of its immense size: Africa is more than three times greater in area than the United States and now includes over fifty independent states.

Nearest the equator are dense tropical rain forests. Large grassy areas known as savannahs lie to the north and south. The trees which dot these landscapes lose their leaves in the dry season. Further to the north and south are deserts: the Sahara in the north, and the Kalahari to the south west. Each of these environments dictates the materials locally available, and consequently affects the nature of the art and crafts produced in each region. Until comparatively recently, direct external influences have been limited to coastal areas, apart from the Cretan influences in the late second millennium BC and those resulting from the brief Assyrian invasion of Egypt in 666 BC.

Egyptian history can be divided into four principal periods, covering 30 dynasties: the Ancient Kingdom (4180 BC – c.3000 BC); the Middle Kingdom (c.3000 BC – 1587 BC); the Modern Kingdom (1587 – 702 BC); the Later Period (664 BC – 525 BC). During the period of the Ancient Kingdom, Memphis was the capital, later replaced by Thebes.

Because of the lack of timber, sunburnt brick was the main building material, although dressed stone was also used for pyramids and statues. Egyptian ornament uses a strictly systematic arrangement of native plants – the lotus-flower, the lily, the papyrus flower, the date-palm. Reeds and maize leaves were also used. Temples represented the world, ceilings the sky, and columns and capitals represented plants. Much decoration is polychromatic. Feathers used for fans and head-dresses were a symbol of sovereignty. As with Assyrian murals, Egyptian art uses flat design to

depict deities, creatures and objects in bas reliefs and paintings. Decorative patterns combine rectilinear forms and undulating scrolls.

The Islamic faith spread throughout Egypt, Syria and Persia. In Syria, North Africa and Persia, the chief characteristics of Islamic art were found towards the close of the eighth century AD; in Egypt, nearly a century later. The naturalistic representation of humans, animals and plants was forbidden, according to the tenets of Islam. This led to the development of purely conventional leaf designs, that often served as backgrounds for Islamic calligraphic inscriptions, and to geometric designs of great variety. Later, the decoration was used for constructional features, such as arches or so-called stalactite vaulting.

The pointed arch was first introduced as an important constructional feature in the Mosque of Ibn Tulun in Cairo in 870 AD. Both horseshoe, four-pointed and cusped (scalloped) arches appear in Islamic architecture. The examples chosen for illustration are predominantly architectural, and demonstrate the wide variety of effects possible in geometric pattern.The interlocking geometric forms of tile patterns influenced the designs of Victorian floor tile manufacturers, and are still suitable for that use today. Floral and foliate patterns are notable for their easy flowing grace. Appearing in carpets and on printed textiles and ceramics, they still remain popular in a traditional context.

The third part of this chapter is concerned with aspects of sub-Saharan African tribal art. Three categories can be distinguished, typifying the various items selected for illustration – symbolic, anecdotal and decorative. The symbolic category includes masks and shields, used in tribal dances and ceremonies. An anecdotal group illustrates the African fondness for animal imagery taken from everyday life. This is sometimes highly stylized, and is often carved on gourds. Bird imagery is also significantly featured. Decorative items include domestic artefacts: vessels and textiles.

African societies traditionally consisted of groups, arranged according to kinship, age grades and secret societies. These were usually religious groups, responsible for ensuring good relations with the spirit world, through masquerades and rituals. They also had economic, military and political functions. Art had, and continues to play, an important social role. Differences in cultural values between one society and another affected whether the work was abstract or figurative.

Masks were worn in religious ceremonies including plays and dances. It was believed that they could manipulate and calm the untamed forces of nature. In many cases they represented spirits living in the forest. By donning a mask and its accompanying fibre or cloth costume, a masquerader came to embody a mythical spirit. Masks were also used in initiation rituals, along with body painting and costumes – marking the passage of boys of a tribe from childhood to adulthood.

Textiles are a very important part of African economy, used for trade, both within the continent and internationally, as well as for clothing and domestic use. Cotton, silk, and raffia are all used, with natural dyes being made from plants. Traditionally, weaving was carried out by both men and women: men used a horizontal loom, while women worked at a vertical loom. Men wove full-time, but women combined weaving with other household duties.

African tribal artefacts began to be collected extensively by Westerners from the late nineteenth century onwards. However, the contexts in which such items were at first acquired – by travellers and hunters, explorers and soldiers – have posed problems of accurate identification and interpretation; a problem common to other aspects of ethnography. More recent case studies based on site-specific careful field work are essential preliminaries for a fuller understanding of the meanings and purposes of African art and artefacts. This point also holds true on a comparative basis for all the other art forms depicted in this encyclopaedia.

THE AMERICAS

North America

The Inuit from Alaska and the far north of Canada are related racially to other groups living in Siberia and in the Aleutian Islands in the Bering Sea. Anthropologists have demonstrated that the Inuit migrated to North America from Siberia, travelling via Beringia, a land bridge in the Bering Straits which would have been open between 25,000 and 10,000 years ago. It has also been suggested that they were part of a larger group which moved southwards via North America and Central America to South America.

The decorative art of the Inuit is largely pictographic – using images to convey cryptic meaning. Frequently, these images are incised on whale bones and walrus tusks. Their simple linear character gives a lively account of daily life among the Inuit.

Like the Inuit, the origin of the native Indians of America is the subject of much speculation. They are thought to have derived from a single people of mixed Asian stock which migrated into North America from Asia via the Bering Straits, during the Upper Pleistocene, that is within the last 50,000 years. Lacking significant contact with the rest of the world, they developed separately, acquiring many different cultures and languages in response to specific geographical and climatic circumstances. Opinions differ as to when they spread through North America and into Central and South America, and how long this process took. One hypothesis suggests that their descendants may have taken 3000 years to reach Tierra del Fuego from North America. By the time Columbus discovered America, the native American population was estimated to be between five and seven million.

Although several Indian artefacts were in European collections by the mid eighteenth century, the specialist study of native Indian arts did not develop until the 1920s. As part of that initiative, a school of design was established at San Ildenfenso, New Mexico, where young Indians were taught to paint traditional Indian patterns. Several of those designs appear in this anthology. North West Coastal Indian artefacts are also included: their imagery is based largely on a system of animal crests expressing their family lineages. Examples illustrated include masks and totem poles.

Around the Great Lakes, the eastern Indians developed considerable skill in embroidered leather work and quillwork. Examples illustrated include mocassins, and tobacco pouches, and a pair of quillwork boxes. In the south west, a sedentary lifestyle emerged, based on irrigation farming. Prior to the arrival of the Spaniards in the sixteenth century, this area was dominated by three local groups: the Mogollon of the Arizona-New Mexico border, the Anasazi of the northern south west, and the Hohokam of the southern desert.

Pottery making and textile technology are thought to have been introduced from nearby Mexico. Between c.700 AD and the Spanish colonization in the sixteenth century the Pueblo culture developed in this region. Along with the typical stone or mud-brick adobe architecture (multi-storeyed, accommodating several families or units), a vigorous local tradition of polychrome pottery was established, that lasted for about 200 years.

Central America

The Central American section of the encyclopaedia includes illustrations of low-relief sculptures from the famous Mayan city of Palenque, rediscovered in the late eighteenth and early nineteenth centuries. The Maya occupied the Yucatan Peninsula, British Honduras, Guatemala, parts of the Mexican states of Tabasco and Chiapas, and the western portions of Honduras and El Salvador. Their culture spanned the period from 1500 BC to 1530 AD, and was at its height between 300 and 900 AD.

The Maya are famous for their remarkable ability in measuring time. They calculated the length of the solar year to be 365.2422 days, and measured a lunar period of 29.5209 days. They measured time from a date zero, August 13, 3113 BC, and believed that the world would end when the Great Cycle of the Long Count ran out on December 24, 2011. They were able to assess the positions of the sun, moon, stars and galaxies.

In pre-Spanish times, they belonged to a larger group known as 'Mesoamerica'. Traits in common among the Mesoamerican Indians included: hieroglyphs; books of bark paper or deerskin folded like screens; a complex permutation calendar; a game played with a rubber ball in a special court; and highly specialized markets in which cocoa beans were used as currency. In their religious ceremonies, they practised self-sacrifice and mutilation, and believed in a pantheon of gods which included a rain god as well as a hero known as the Feathered Serpent, Quetzacoatl. They also believed in a multitiered heaven and underworld, and a universe oriented to the four directions with specified colours and gods assigned to the cardinal points and to the centre.

South America

The South American imagery testifies to the survival of native craft traditions in wood carving, textiles, metalwork and ceramics, using manual skills and local materials, often without significant mechanization. Zoomorphic (animal-based) imagery features strongly.

Spanish colonialization from the sixteenth century had a rather devastating effect on local traditional crafts, by imposing European tastes and production methods. With textiles, it was only in more remote areas of the highlands or in tropical lowlands that much of the traditional way of life was retained. Indigenous textiles are woven using drop spindles and backstrap looms. They use warp-faced weaves, the only Peruvian textile technique that has survived from the third millennium BC, to create colourful striped woollen cloths with banded traditional geometric patterns.

Details from Tiahuanaco (now known as Tiwanaco), Bolivia's most important archaeological site, are also illustrated. Located near Lake Titicaca, it was once the centre of one of the most ancient cultures in the Americas, the Aymara Indians, which lasted from c.600 BC to c.1200 AD, when it was conquered by the Incas. The Gate of the Sun was thought to be a solar calendar and forms part of an elaborate observatory and courtyard containing monoliths, the door of the Puma, and a subterranean temple.

AUSTRALASIA

The final chapter presents a selection of images from the art of the Pacific, including the Hawaiian Islands to the north of the central Pacific, Australia and New Zealand in the south west, and the three groups of islands: Micronesia, Melanesia and Polynesia. Micronesia includes the Cook and Gilbert Islands, and lies to the west, just north of the Equator; Melanesia in the south west Pacific includes Papua New Guinea, the Solomon Islands and the New Hebrides; Polynesia in the South Pacific includes Tahiti, the Tuamotu Archipelago and the Marquesas.

The area is vast, and its history of settlement and cultures diverse. Its pre-European and pre-American population derives from two physical types: Australoid and Mongoloid. Australoid people moved into New Guinea from Indonesia about 100,000 years ago. Australia was settled around 40,000 years ago. Australoid people had turned to some form of agriculture by the end of the last glacial period (c.9000 BC). Linguistic fragmentation occurred, as result of divergence in settlement (there are about forty languages in Australia, and more than four hundred separate languages in New Guinea).

Mongoloid types can be traced to South East Asia and perhaps south China. The Austranesian family of languages derived from them is spoken in South East Asia, Indonesia, Melanesia, Micronesia and Polynesia. The last great movement prior to the arrival of Europeans occurred c.3000 BC when a small group speaking an Austranesian language – ancestors of the Polynesians – developed the out-rigger canoe and the art of sea voyaging, and gradually moved into all the islands from the Solomons to the New Hebrides. They were traders and farmers, and also produced a very fine stamped pottery called Lapita, named after the site in New Caledonia where it was first found. Pottery finds trace patterns of settlement: c.2000 BC in New Caledonia and Fiji; in Tonga and Samoa c.1000 BC; sometime before 700 AD in the islands of the eastern Pacific, settled by canoe from Samoa.

Early collecting occurred haphazardly, by explorers, traders, seal-hunters, whalers and missionaries. Christian missionaries went to Polynesia in the nineteenth century. In Melanesia, the change to Christianity and tourist carving has happened much more recently, during this century. In these instances, it is almost impossible to understand work in its original social context, except with recent pieces.

The Australian aborigines are nomads, whose native way of life recalls the Stone Age. Their mythology informs their art, which plays an integral part in community life, used by tribal magicians to control the forces of nature, increase food supply, punish wrong-doers or destroy enemies. Aborigines believe in the 'Dream-time', an ill-defined period in the past when giant semi-human figures created the topography of the Australian landscape. They also believe that prior to any life, the earth had always existed as a flat, featureless plain, stretching to the edges of the universe. Aboriginal art consists of engraving, sculpture and painting, with the latter predominant.

Different styles evolved in different parts of the continent. Some of the most dramatic images are found in Arnhem land, in the Northern Territory. Shields, boomerangs and spear-throwers were engraved; sculptured and modelled figures of men and animals were widely spread throughout Australia. The paintings of the Australian aborigines were executed on weapons and implements, on the ground at the time of certain totemic ceremonies, on burial poles and as body decoration on mourners, and on rocks in caves and on bark. Many of the rock and bark paintings represent spirit figures, both malevolent and kind, who it was thought could be invoked through the paintings.

Elsewhere in the Pacific, carving and weaving are more predominant art forms, partly because of local materials, partly because of their portability. Both native woods, shells, and, in New Zealand, a form of green soapstone, were used for carvings. Headdresses and costumes were woven and constructed from feathers and grasses, the latter often woven in complex patterns. Carvings vary from totemic figures, which are sometimes starkly dramatic, to intricate patterns of incised ornament, used for ceremonial paddles, spears and clubs. Art forms in Polynesia had several symbolic functions: to communicate, to convey legends or to depict founding ancestors, and to increase the 'mana' (prestige) of the possessor.

By drawing on designs from civilizations and cultures from around the world, the main aim of this fascinating encyclopaedia is to increase an awareness and understanding of traditional art forms. Due to the limitations of space, the selection concentrates on the designs of indigenous peoples. The images are all pre-twentieth century and have been chosen to reveal designs that may have fallen out of common usage over time, motifs from unusual sources and patterns that reflect the rich creativity of ancient cultures.

With informative captions picking out stylistic details, the pages of this book will enthrall practising artists and designers and students of art history, archaeology and anthropology, along with anyone interested in geography, history and ethnography, making it an essential sourcebook.

EUROPE

ANCIENT CRETAN ORNAMENT

Egyptian and Assyrian influence is apparent in these examples of Cretan ornament, ranging in date from c1800 to c1200 BC. Sources include examples of Cretan pottery from the British Museum *above left,* and coins and jewels excavated by Schliemann at Mycenae *below left and right.* Note the strong use of the spiral.

GREEK ORNAMENT

Architectural ornament in the Doric style, 1104 to 470 BC, and *opposite* in the Ionic style, 470 to 338 BC. Note the use of the honeysuckle and egg-and-dart motifs, and the Ionic volutes *opposite lower left.* Sources include the Parthenon (Doric), and the temples dedicated to Apollo Didymaeus at Miletus and Minerva Pallas at Priene (Ionic).

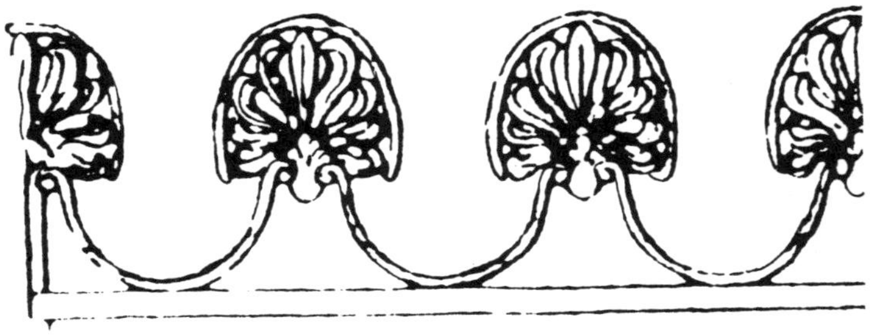

GREEK ORNAMENT

The Corinthian style (338 to 146 BC) marks the last independent phase of Greek ornament, prior to its merging with the Roman style. More decorative and elaborate than the Doric or Ionic styles, it also focuses on architectural ornament. Sources here include the Lysicrates Monument and the Tower of the Winds, both in Athens.

GREEK ORNAMENT

Top left and top right echinus and astragal mouldings from the Erechtheion (British Museum). *Left column, t–b* anthemion, Greek key and guilloche patterns. Spirals from Greek terracotta *centre right*, and from a tomb at Mycenae, Argolis, *bottom right*. *Left* Ionic volutes above a palmette motif, from the Antefix of the Parthenon.

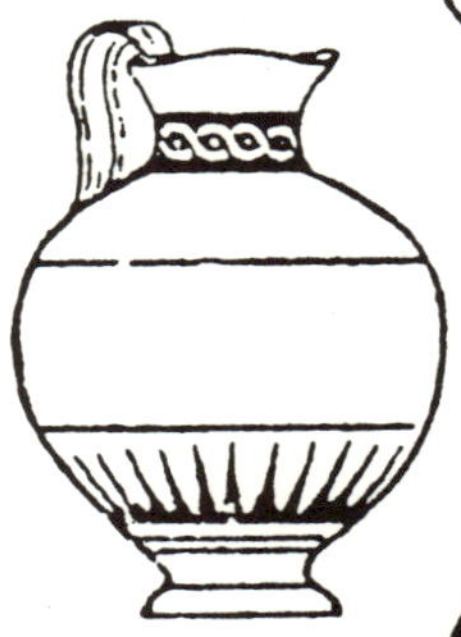

GREEK CERAMICS

Greek ceramics were produced between c1000 BC and 300 BC. Examples on *this page* show the later types of Attic black coloured vessels, dating from the 6th century BC onwards. *Opposite top right* a vase from the island of Mytilene, c1000 BC; *bottom right* a vase on a tripod base from Boetta.

GREEK ORNAMENT

The Greek key pattern, known also as the meander or fret, appears in many forms, some more complex than others. Applications vary widely, from architectural friezes to tile and wall patterns and applied motifs on furniture and textiles, ceramics and metalwork. Both the Greek key pattern and palmette motifs *top right* lend themselves to stencil decoration.

VASE ORNAMENT

A variety of details of border ornament, from Greek and Etruscan vases in the British Museum and the Louvre. Ornament was applied by an embossed roller, suitably primed, with slip (liquid clay) being pressed round the outside of the vessel to be decorated.

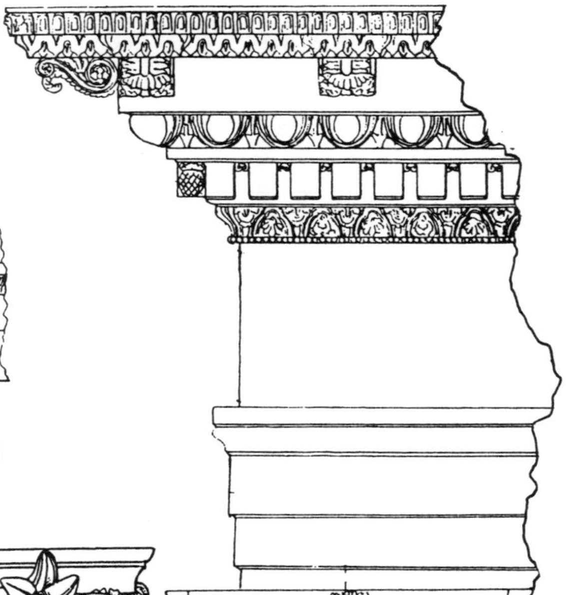

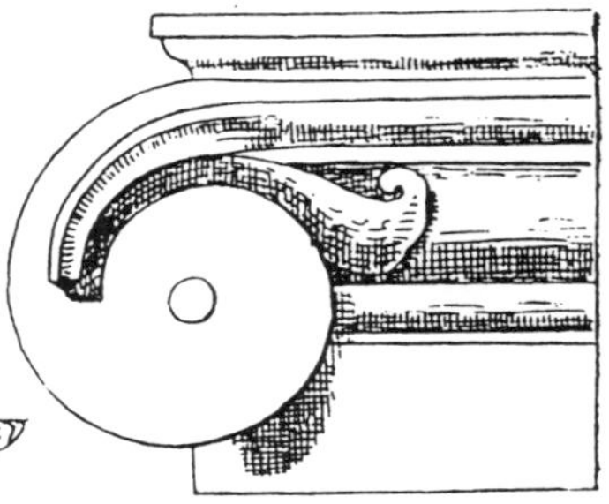

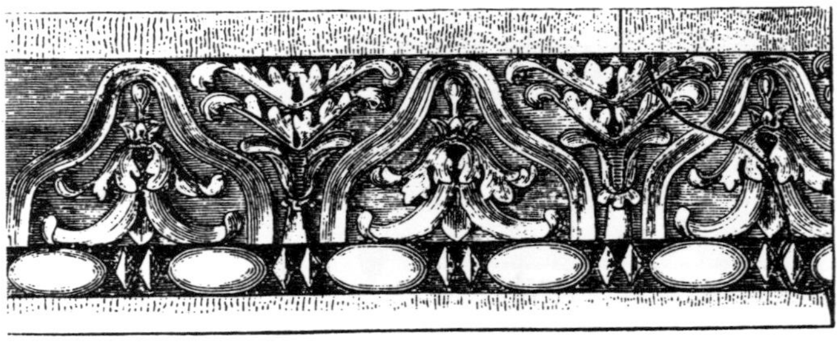

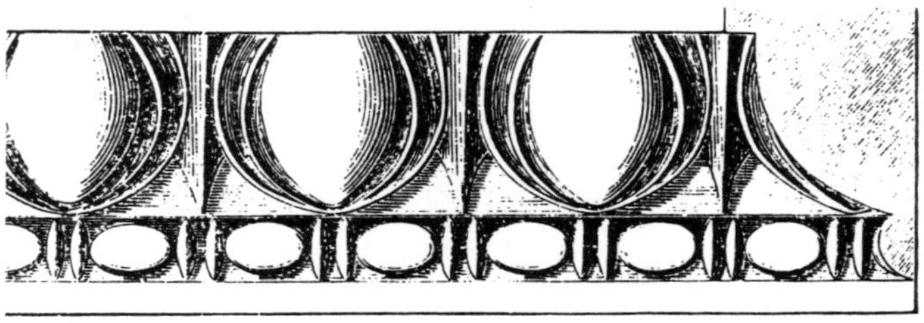

ROMAN ARCHITECTURAL DETAILS

Entablatures, friezes, capitals, columns and their bases. The Roman composite order, seen here, combined Ionic and Corinthian styles of capitals. Mouldings show uses of acanthus leaf, guilloche and egg-and-dart mouldings. Illustrations include the capital and entablature *this page, top right* from the interior of the Parthenon in Rome.

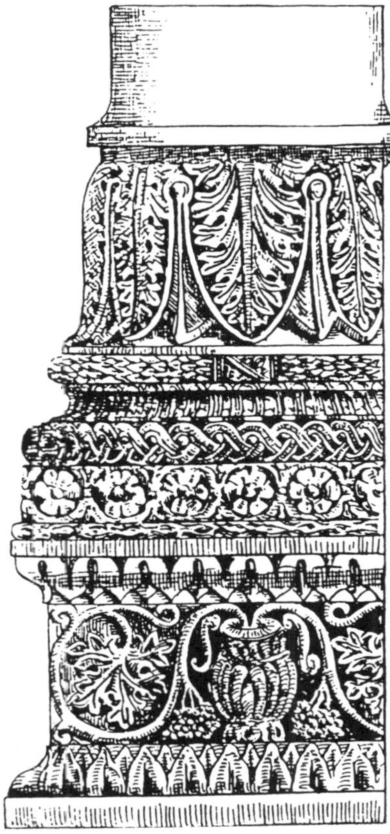
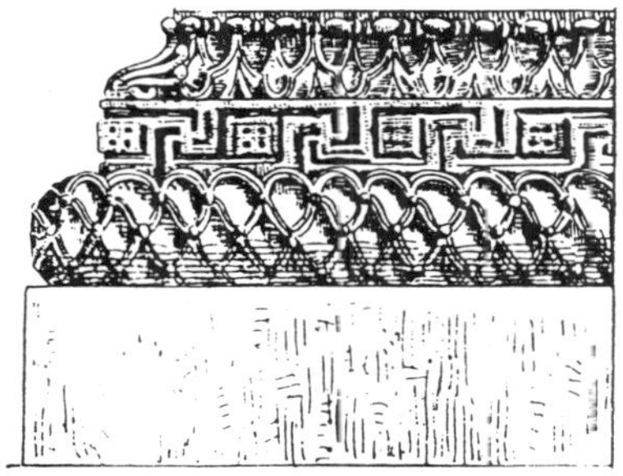
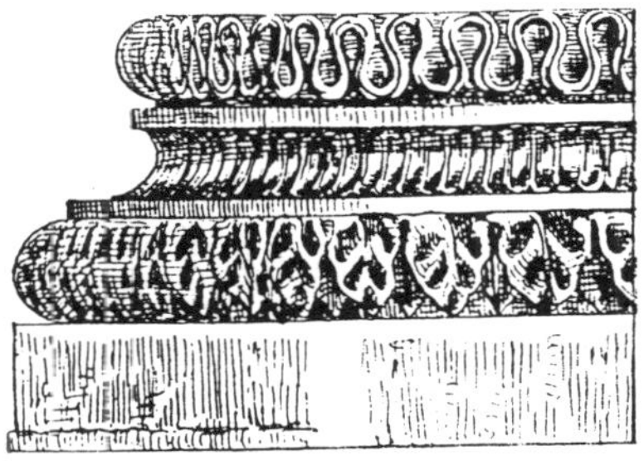
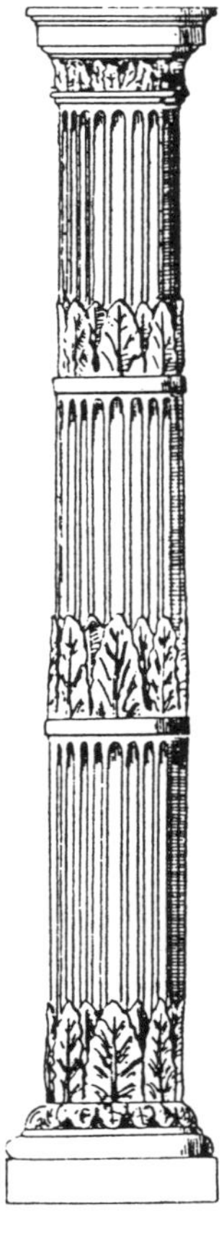
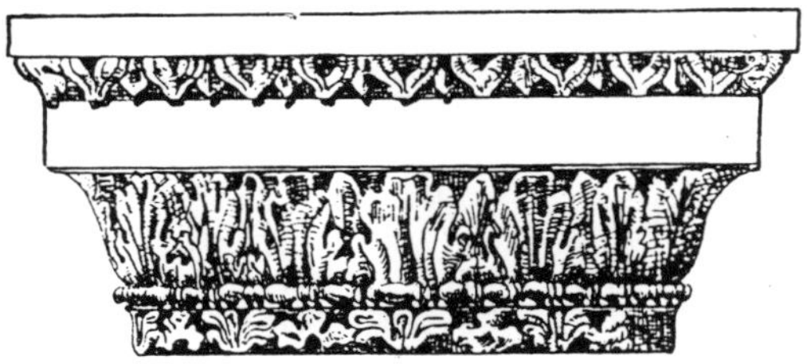

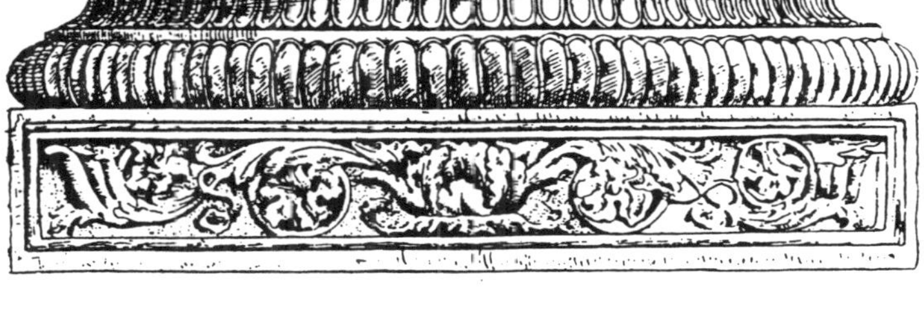

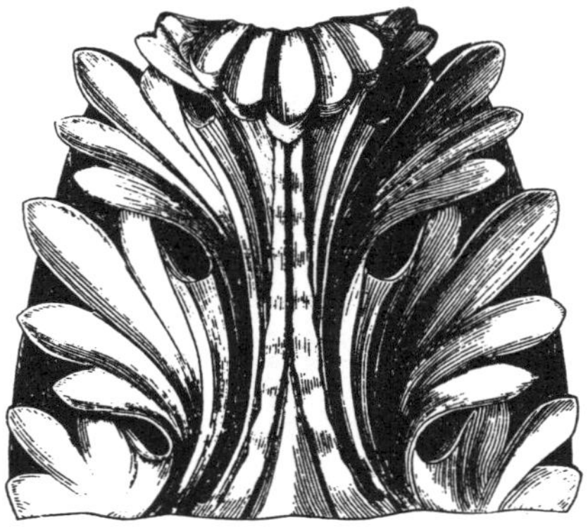

ROMAN ARCHITECTURAL ORNAMENT

The acanthus leaf is widely used in Roman architectural ornament, as low relief decoration, in friezes, and capitals. The tympanum *top right* is carved in white marble (Mattei Palace, Rome).

ROMAN ARCHITECTURAL ORNAMENT: CORINTHIAN AND COMPOSITE CAPITALS

Sources: *top, l–r* Temple of Jupiter Stator, Rome; Temple of Vesta, Tivoli; Arch of Constantine, Rome; *middle, l–r* Arch of Trajan, Ancona; Arch of Titus, Rome; *bottom, l–r* Temple of Mars Victor, Rome and Pantheon, Rome; *left* Pantheon and Arch of Septimus Severus, Rome.

USE OF ANIMALS IN ROMAN PATTERN

Animals figure strongly in Roman decorative carvings. Above fragment of an antique frieze found at Tivoli. *Opposite lower left* rams' heads on a marble altar (Villa Borghese, Rome). Other pictures show mythological creatures such as griffons, as in fragments from the Forum of Trajan, Rome.

POMPEIAN ORNAMENT

Pompeii, near Naples, subject to Rome from the 4th century BC, was a popular luxury summer resort until destroyed by a volcano in AD 79. Excavations beginning in 1748 revealed its sophisticated style, combining Greek and Roman influences. Examples illustrated include architectural ornament, bronzes, murals and mosaics.

BYZANTINE DECORATION

Byzantine decoration synthesizes Classical Roman and Oriental influences. *Top* 6thC fretwork marble screens from Ravenna. Sources for the tesselated pavements *opposite* include the basilica of Sta Maria in Cosmedin, Rome, and the Palatine Chapel, Palermo. Note the leather case *centre right,* with its decorative use of animals.

BYZANTINE SURFACE PATTERN

Details of 12th and 13thC mosaic decoration from the Italian Cathedrals of Ravello and Monreale, and the Ziza and Palatine chapels, Palermo. Details from a jewelled gospel book cover from The Louvre *right* illustrate the Byzantine taste for rich effects.

MARCVS
ECCEMA
TER
+BEATRIX MEI HONORE
DEI O

BYZANTINE ORNAMENT

Decorative strapwork used in Byzantine low relief marble sculptural ornament. *Opposite upper right* decorative details from Byzantine illuminated manuscripts (Bibliothèque Nationale, Paris). *Opposite bottom left* frieze over door of the Zeno Chapel, St Mark's, Venice.

BYZANTINE SCULPTURE

Low relief sculptural ornament, selected primarily from two of the greatest Byzantine buildings, the basilicas of Sta Sophia, Constantinople (now Istanbul), and St Mark, Venice. Byzantine marble cushion capitals vary quite widely in form. The drill is frequently used for undercutting, giving a lacy pierced effect to the design.

EARLY CHRISTIAN ORNAMENT

A selection from early Christian illuminated manuscripts (7th to 11th centuries) including the Book of Durrow and the Lindisfarne Gospels. The style is also used for sculpture, as on the Aberlemno stone *opposite bottom centre,* a slab with an elaborate low relief cross from Angus, Scotland.

CELTIC METALWORK

From the 5th century BC, the Celts spread westwards from central Europe, settling as far as Ireland. They were renowned for their high quality metalwork, which diplays chasing, embossing, engraving and enamelling techniques. All the bronzes shown are British, except the mirror *above* from Nijmegen, Holland. Many are items of body armour.

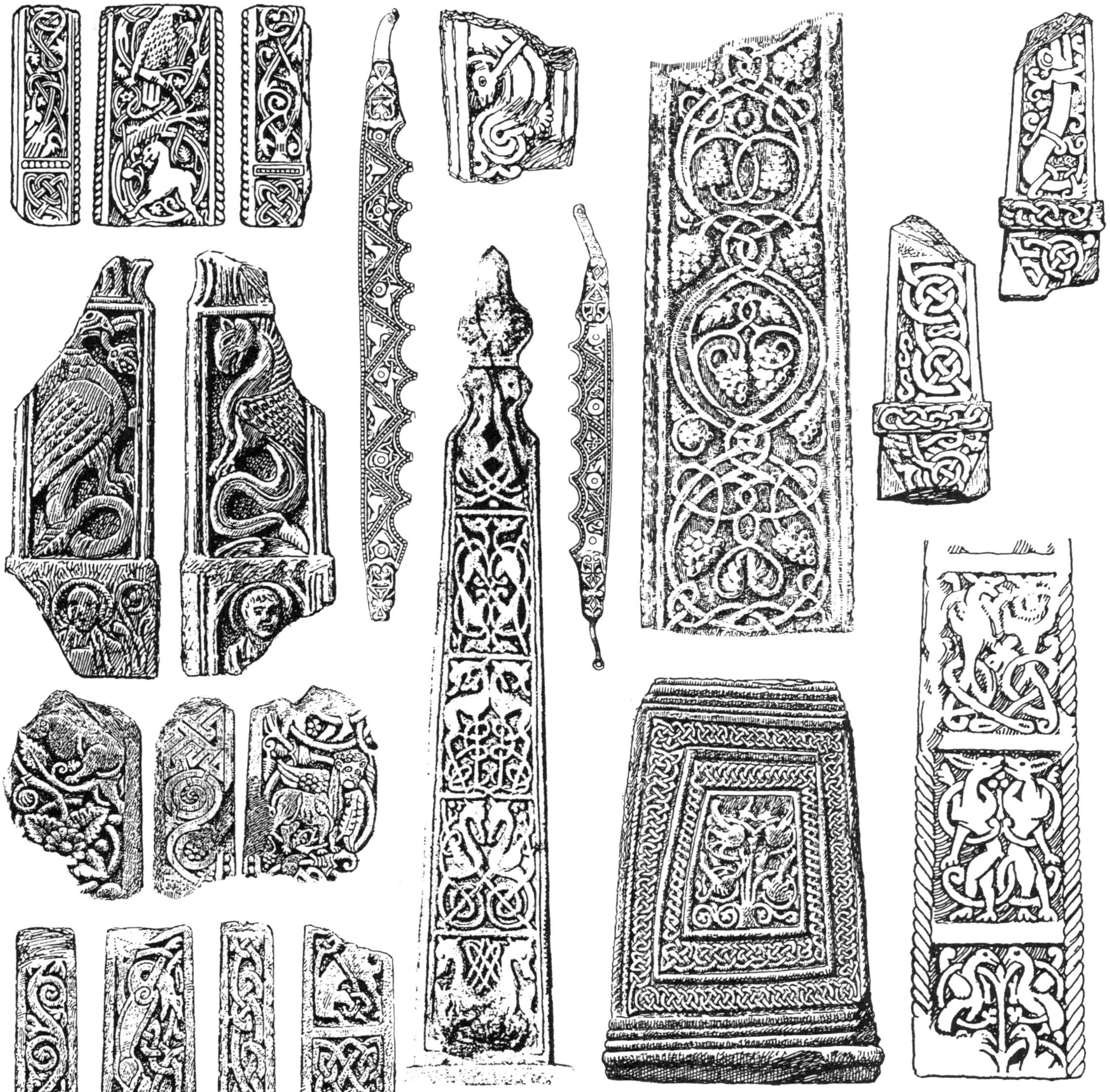

ANGLO-SAXON ORNAMENT

All except two illustrations are 7th to 9thC fragments of stone crosses from the north of England, combining Celtic interlace with early Christian imagery, e.g. saints or vine scrolls. The exceptions are two scallop edged silver and niello strap mounts *top centre,* part of a hoard found at Trewiddle, Cornwall, dating from 900 AD.

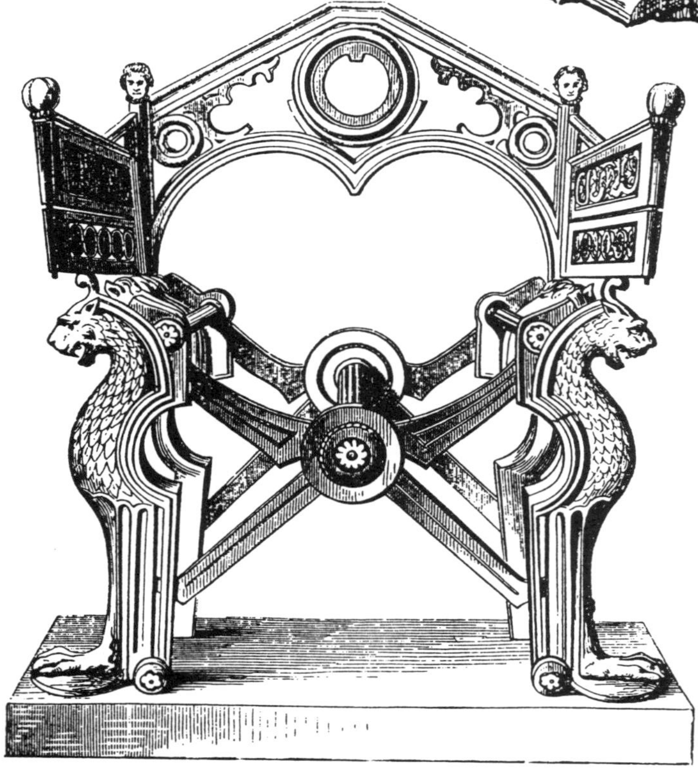

FRANKISH AND CAROLINGIAN METALWORK AND MANUSCRIPT ILLUMINATION

Charlemagne ruled as Holy Roman Emperor from 800 to 814 AD. *Top left* detail of pommel of his ceremonial sword. *Right* the Throned Christ, from one of his Gospel books. *Above* the gilt bronze Curule chair of Dagobert, King of the Franks, closely based on a Roman campaign stool; the back and sides are 12thC.

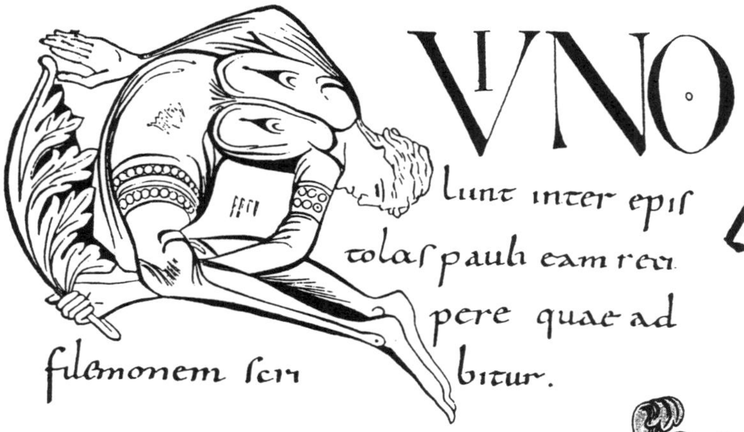

EARLY MEDIEVAL MANUSCRIPT ILLUMINATION

A selection of English and French manuscript illumination (9th to 11th centuries) displays the lingering influence of Celtic interlace, combined with foliate ornament. The large 'B' centre is from a Latin Psalter (British Library).

FRENCH ROMANESQUE SCULPTURE

A selection of Romanesque sculpture taken from fragments and capitals in the Museum of Toulouse *above and right,* dating from the 11th to 13th centuries. Unusually, Moorish and Christian influences are combined in the capital *this page top right* with its scalloped canopy and honeycomb background, both Moorish inspired, providing a setting for the Christian scene of the Flight from Egypt.

FRENCH ROMANESQUE SCULPTURE

Bold execution and dramatic imagery are characteristics of French Romanesque sculpture. All except one of the details shown are from the Notre Dame Cathedral, Poitiers, dating from the 12th century. The dado from St Gilles *centre right,* featuring a centaur chasing a hart, may be an allegory representing the Devil attempting to catch a soul.

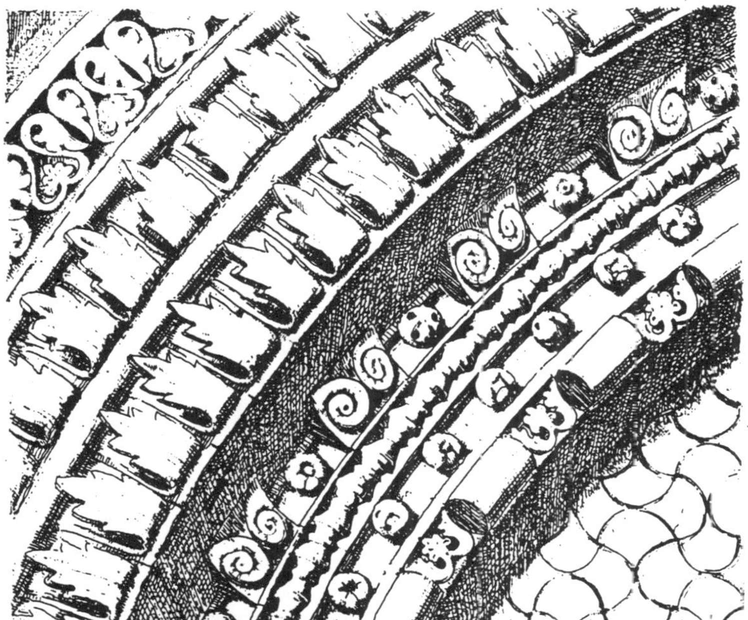

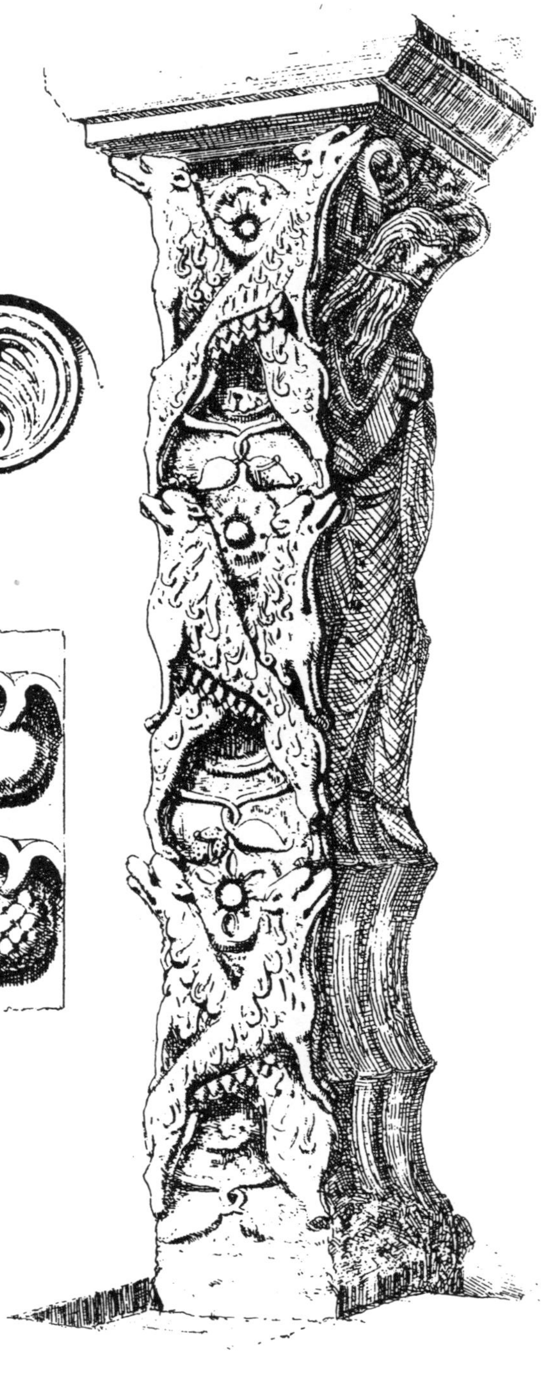

FRENCH ROMANESQUE SCULPTURE

Outstanding details from the Abbey Church of Moissac: the central pier of the portal (main entrance) *above right*, dates from the early 12th century. Symbolic lions and lionesses representing Christ and the Church are flanked by figures of St Peter and St Paul, to whom the church is dedicated. The capital *above left* is from the cloister.

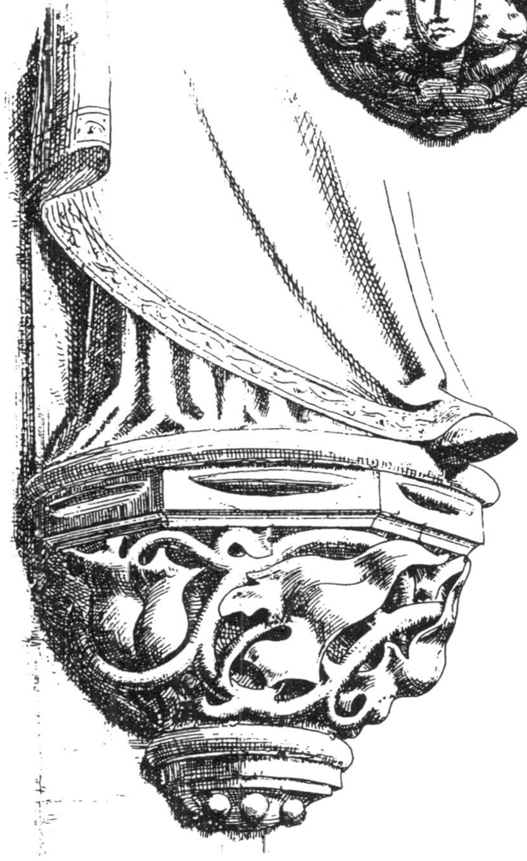

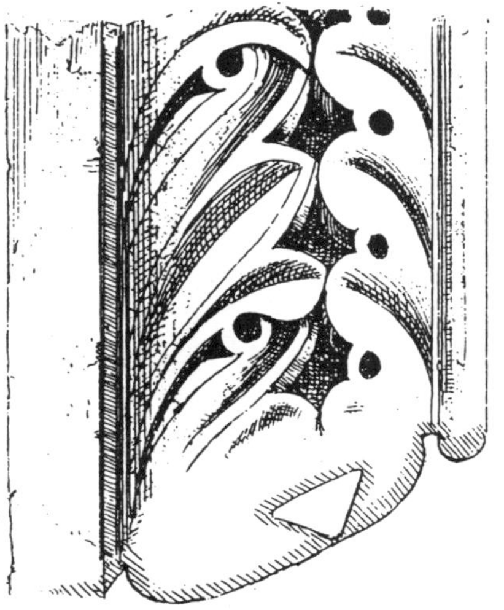

SPANISH ROMANESQUE AND GOTHIC SCULPTURE

Examples of medieval sculpture from Spain show contrasting styles of carving, from the use of undercutting and drilling in the Romanesque cloisters of Las Huelgas, near Burgos, to the sinuous grace of foliate ornament on a bracket *above left* from San Juan, Toledo.

ITALIAN ROMANESQUE MOSAICS AND SCULPTURE

Examples from Sicily and central Italy. The Sicilian mosaics *this page* are from the Palantine Chapel, Palermo and *centre and bottom right* from Monreale and Messina Cathedrals. Amongst sculpture from the cathedrals of Genoa, Lucca, Pisa and Volterra *opposite,* note two capitals from Nicola Pisano's pulpit in Pisa Cathedral *top left.*

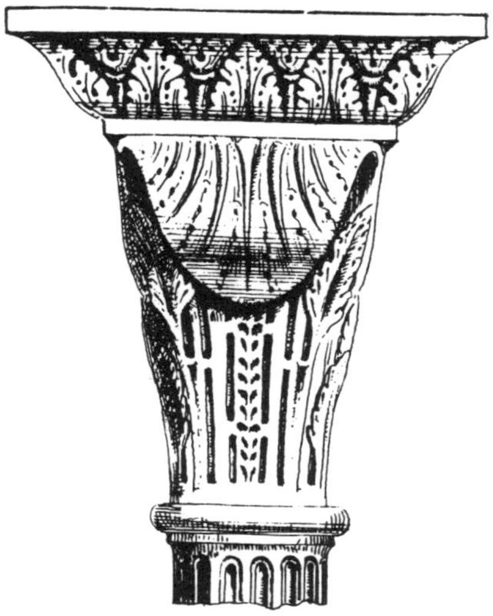

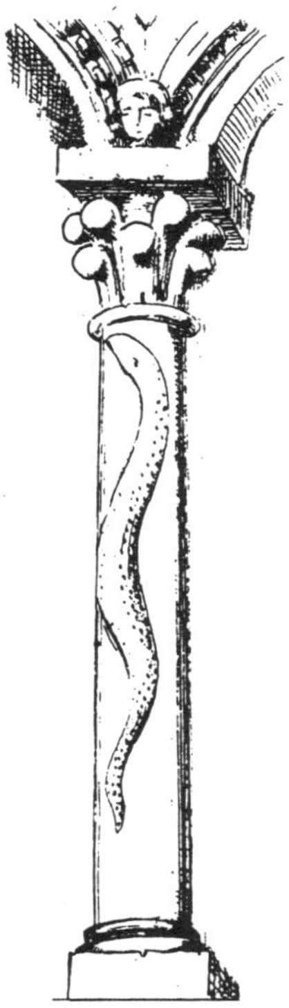

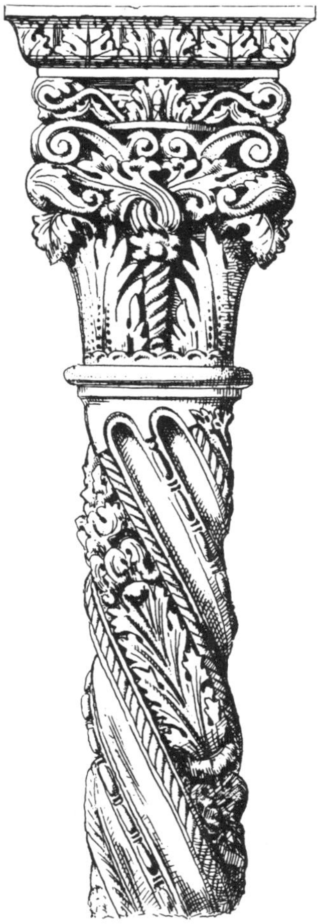

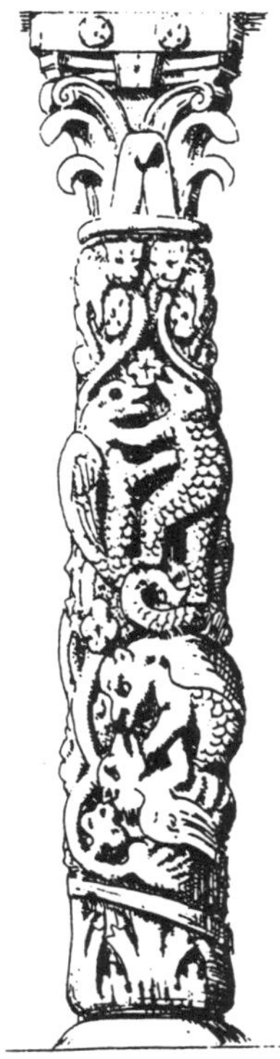

18EW65

GERMAN ROMANESQUE SCULPTURE, METALWORK AND MANUSCRIPTS

German Romanesque ecclesiastical decoration of the 11th and 12th centuries is noted for its rich quality and variety. Palmettes and scrolls feature strongly. *Opposite top* a portion of the bronze corona from Hildesheim Cathedral. *Opposite left* a cherubim from the Mauricius Shrine in Cologne Cathedral, c1180, showing the use of champlevé enamel.

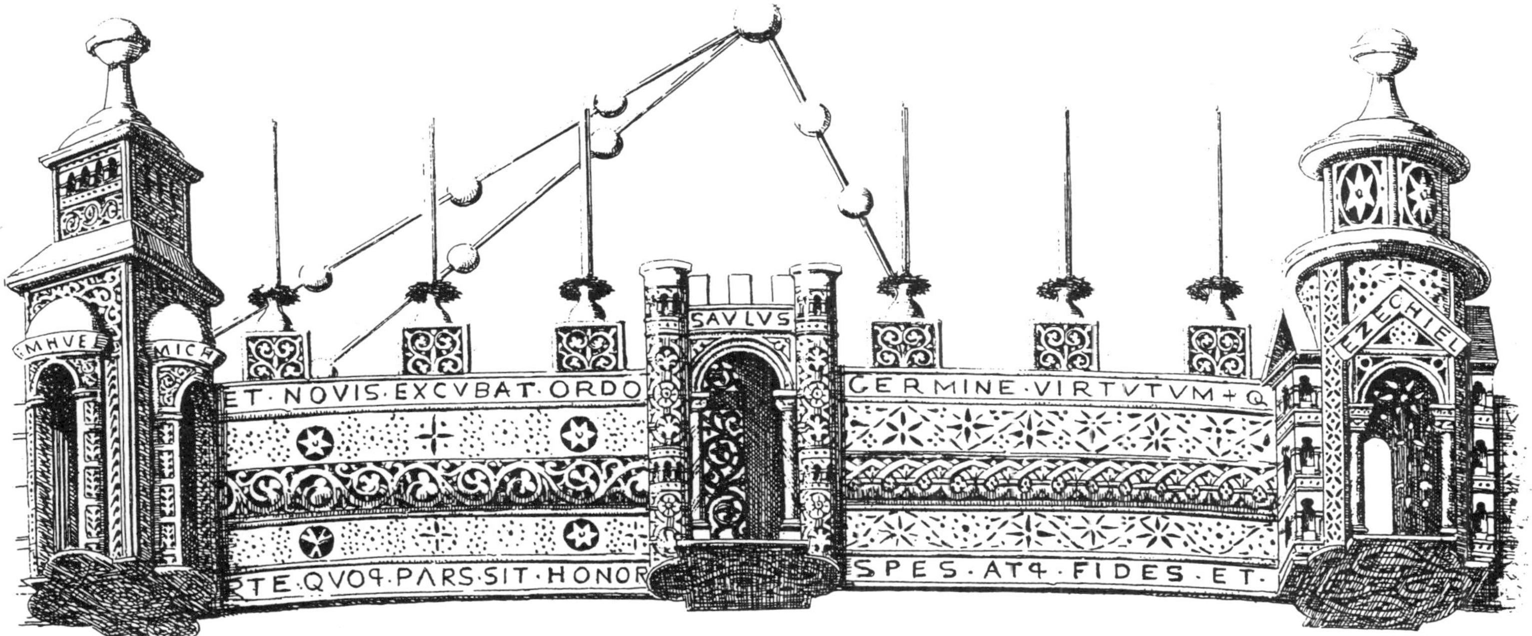
EMHVE
MICH
SAVLVS
EZECHIEL
ET·NOVIS·EXCVBAT·ORDO
GERMINE·VIRTVTVM+Q
RTE·QVOꝗ·PARS·SIT·HONOR
SPES·ATꝗ·FIDES·ET·

CHERUBIN

REXIT HE

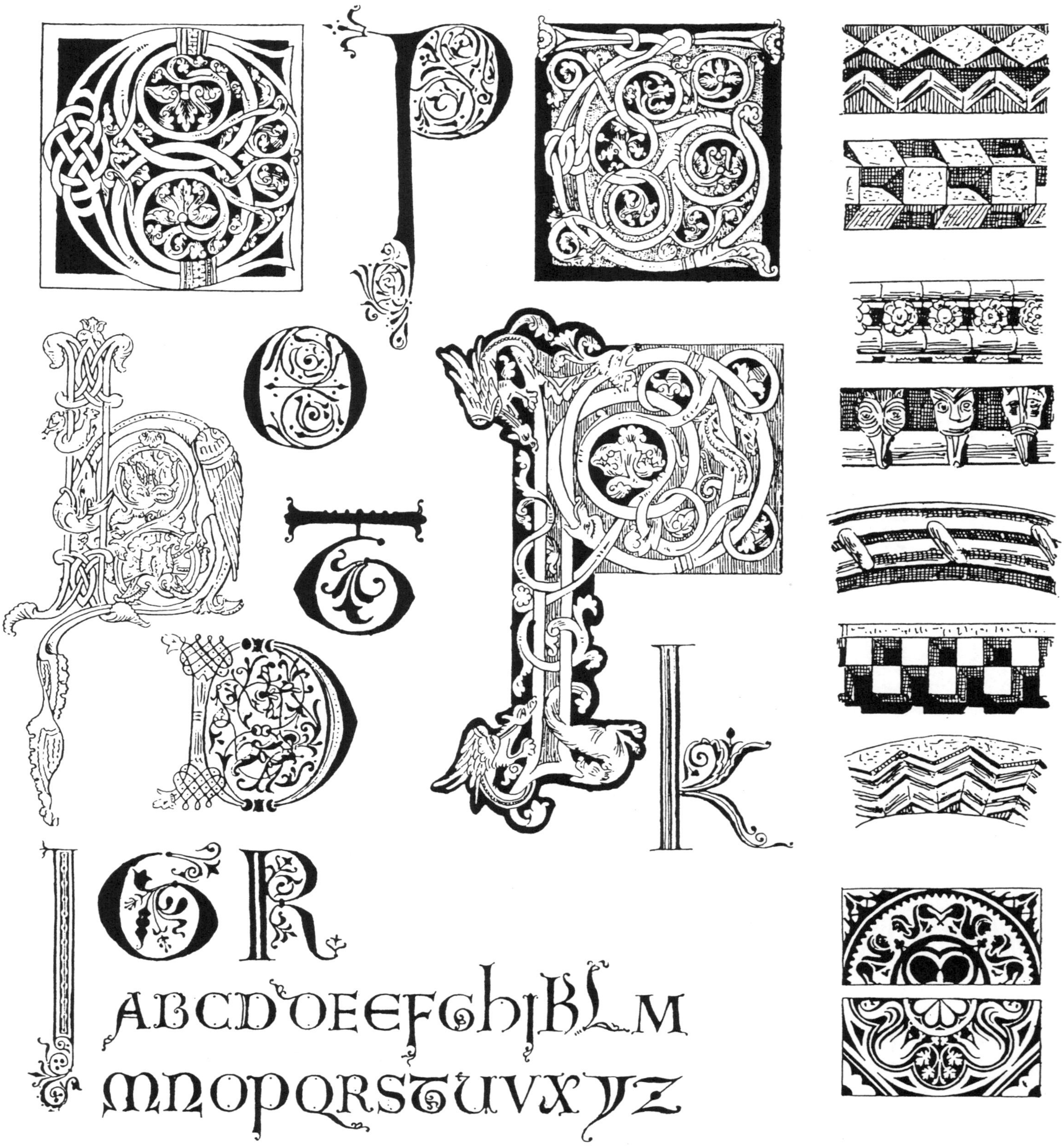

ENGLISH ROMANESQUE ORNAMENT

A selection of English Romanesque ornament from manuscript illumination, tiles, sculpture and architectural details. The manuscript initials (British Library), still display the use of interlace and occasional fantastical animals. But like the low relief panels from St Saviour's Church, Southwark, *opposite,* they also use scrollwork. Architectural details *opposite* include examples from Canterbury, Peterborough and Rochester Cathedrals. The font *opposite centre right* is from Winchester Cathedral.

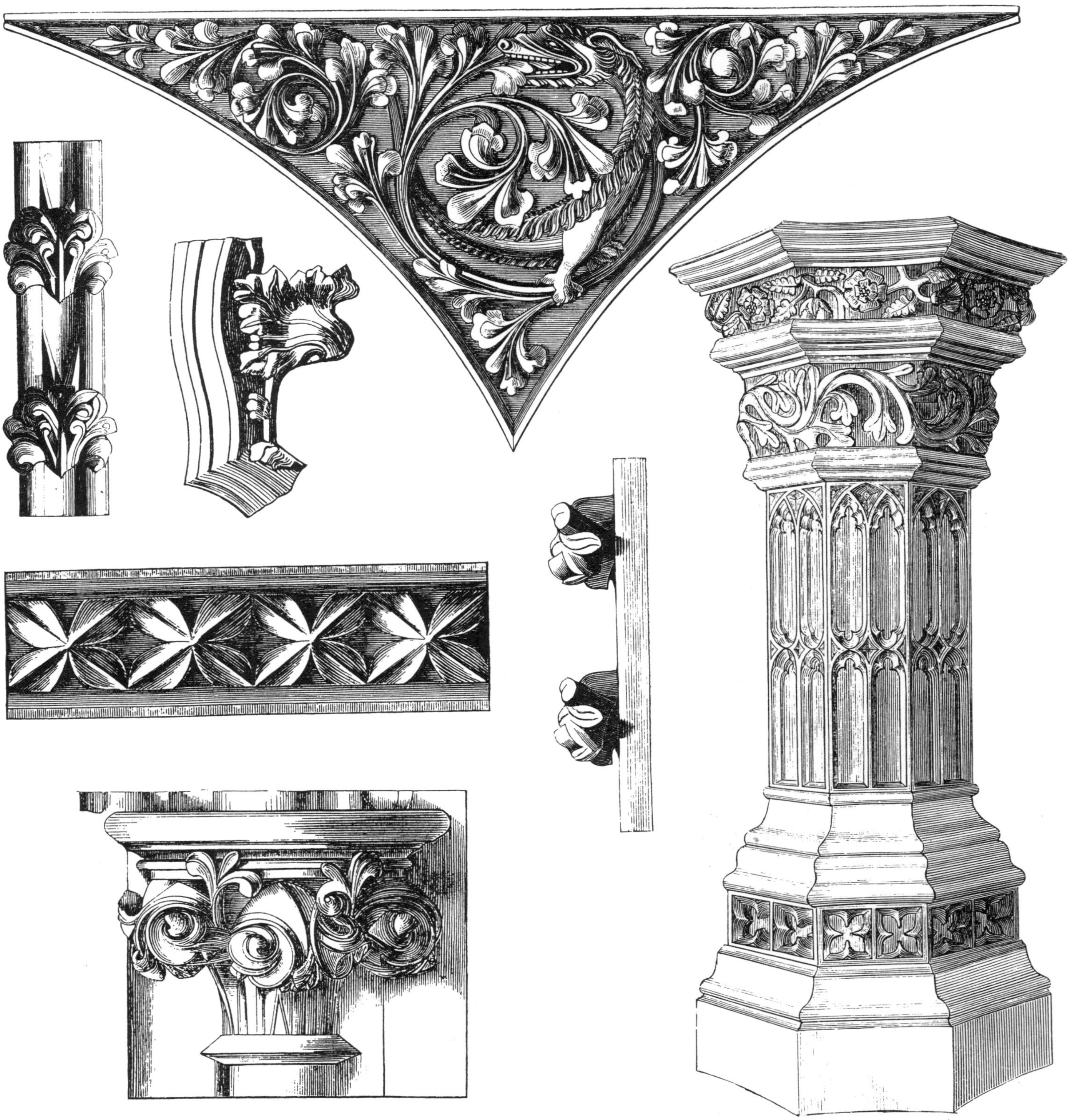

GOTHIC ARCHITECTURAL ORNAMENT

The Gothic style began to evolve from the Romanesque in France in the 12th century, spreading rapidly to Italy, Germany, Spain, England and elsewhere. Three vertical details *this page* of stone crockets from Lincoln Cathedral, the stiff leaf capitals *above left* from the Temple Church, London, and French examples from churches at Sens and Nevers *top and above right.* Woodwork is sometimes naturalistic *opposite centre left;* sometimes more formal, as in the use of cusped arches.

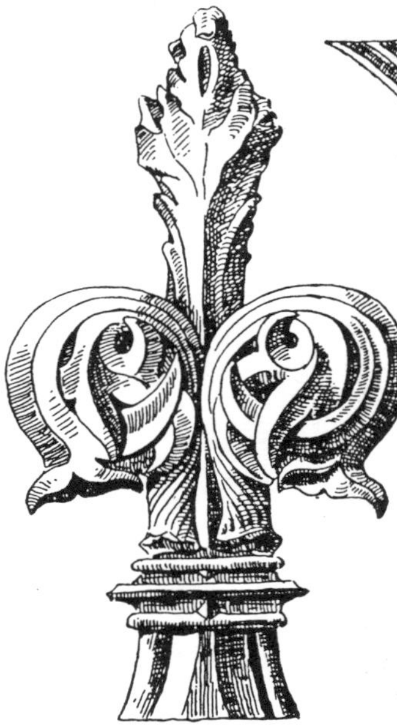

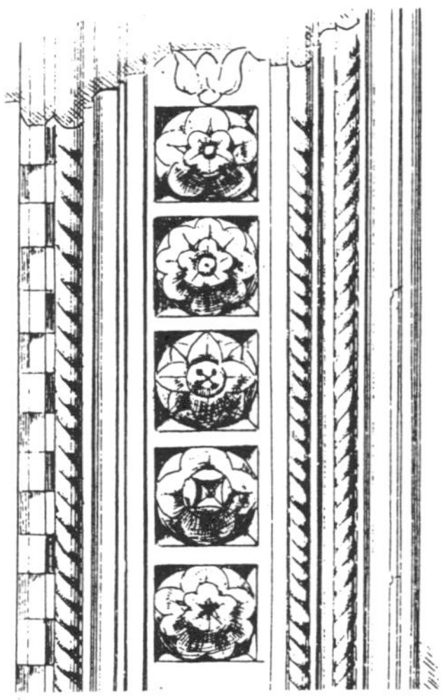

GOTHIC ORNAMENT

Further details of Gothic sculpture show how the style varies and is used for both secular and religious decoration. Acanthus leaves can still be found *second column, centre* but more often other leaves are adapted to the 'stiff leaf' style. Sources include *top right* wood carvings from the stalls of the Church of San Zeno, Verona; *bottom right* Hotel Cluny, Paris. The vine scroll column *opposite extreme right* is from the Royal Miraflores monuments, Spain.

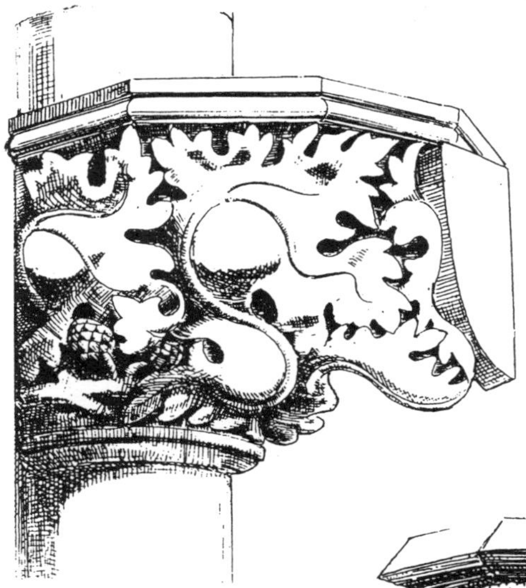

GOTHIC METALWORK

Security is an important reason for the use of architectural metalwork: usually bronze or iron. Seen here is a variety of hinges, finials, locks and door knockers, together with *opposite* several details of mouldings and finials. The art of the locksmith and blacksmith reached new heights throughout Europe during the Gothic period, thanks in part to the rigorous three-stage practical apprenticeship still pursued under the Craft Guild system. Metal techniques used here include forging, casting, piercing and chasing.

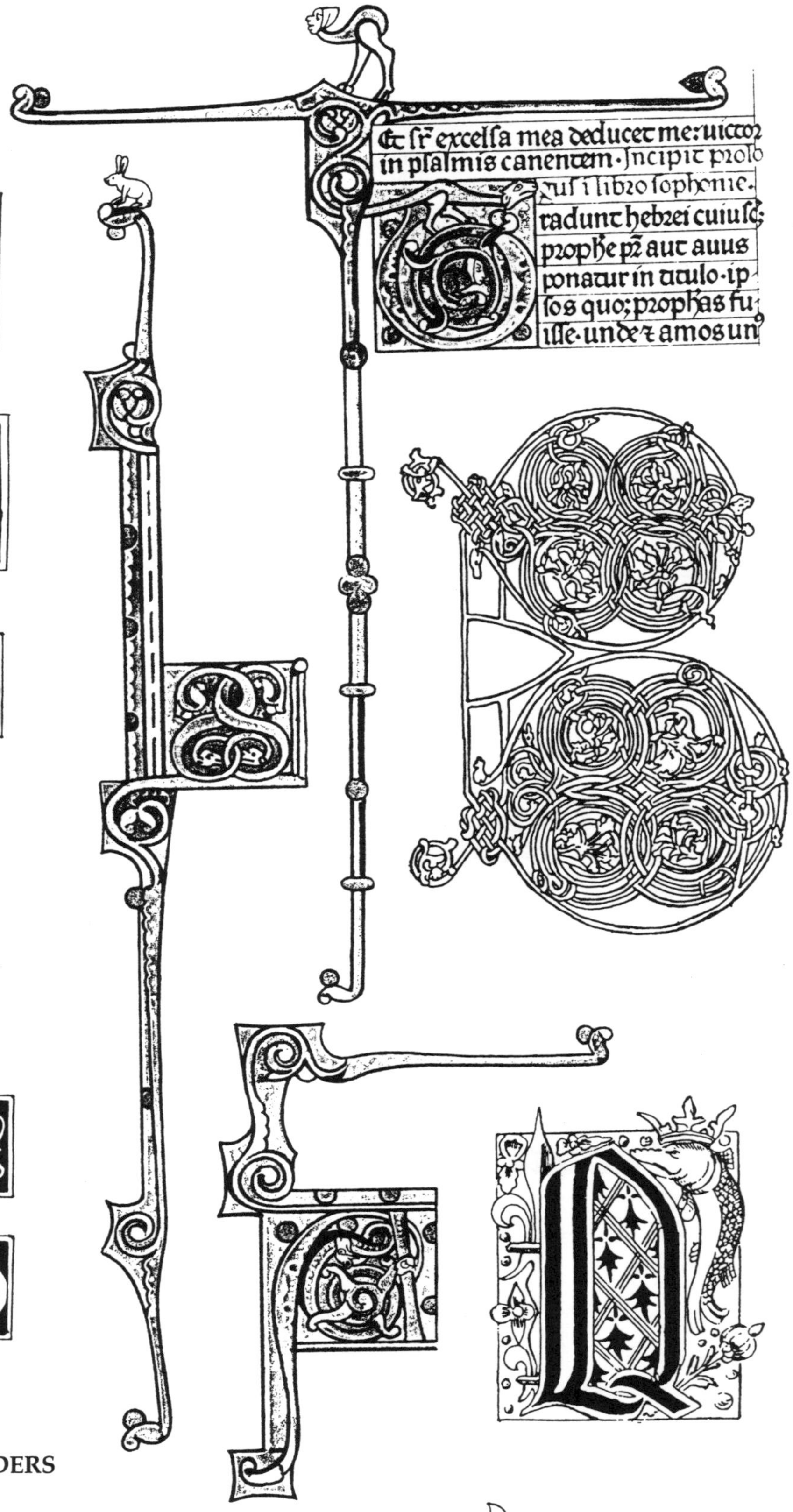

GOTHIC LETTERING AND DECORATIVE BORDERS

The Gothic style of letters with its characteristic strong vertical emphasis and italic form lends itself to use for manuscript and printed texts and engraved inscriptions, as in the examples from German 15th and early 16thC bronze tomb-plates *opposite right.*

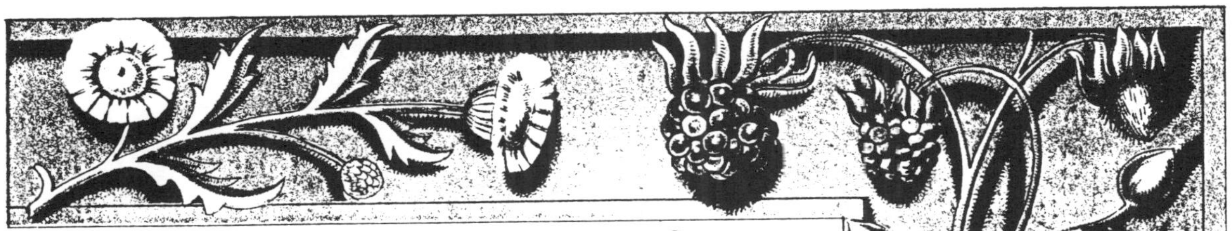

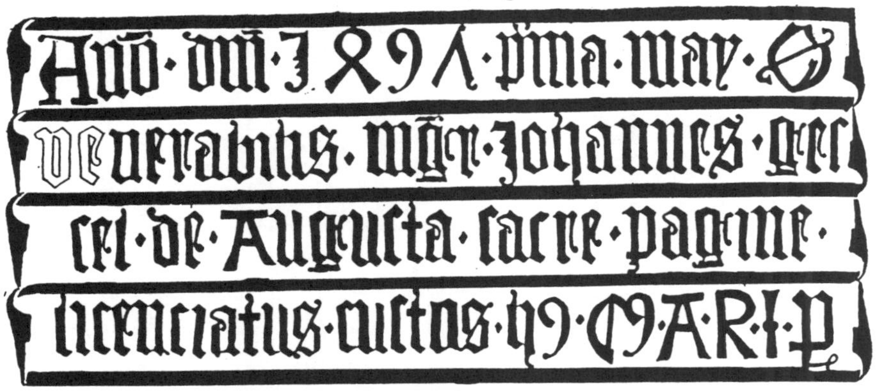

GOTHIC PATTERN

A selection of designs for flat pattern, reinterpreted from illuminated manuscripts in the Bibliothèque Nationale, Paris. The designs are predominantly formal in character and would originally have been used for a variety of purposes, ranging from woven silk, woollen and cut velvet textiles, wall stencils and murals to embossed leather.

GOTHIC STAINED GLASS

Examples of French and German stained glass using a part-monochrome, part-coloured technique known as grisaille. The sources are Bourges, Chartres, Cologne, Strasbourg and Tournai Cathedrals. Contrast the examples from Cologne Cathedral *top two rows* begun 1248, with those from Tournai Cathedral *bottom left and right* dating from between 1475 and 1500.

MOORISH ARCHITECTURE AND TILES

Examples of Moorish architectural ornament and tile patterns, taken from the Alhambra, Granada, and Alcazar, Seville. Both are major monuments of Islamic architecture built during the Moorish occupation of southern Spain between the 8th and 12th centuries. Moorish ornament displays remarkable facility in the organization of surface pattern, interweaving and interlacing geometric and arabesque forms; human depiction was forbidden, according to the tenets of the Islamic faith.

MOORISH ORNAMENT

A selection of motifs in the Moorish style, created by the Victorian designer and historian John Leighton and originally published by him. They display both geometric and foliate ornament. Sources include the Alhambra, Granada.

HUNGARIAN EMBROIDERY

Hungary is especially noted for the range and quality of its embroidery. The example shown *above*, with its stylized, geometric characters, is for execution in needlepoint, on linen or canvas, and would be suitable for an oblong table, mat or cushion. The examples of borders *opposite* use a variety of stitches, including satin stitch.

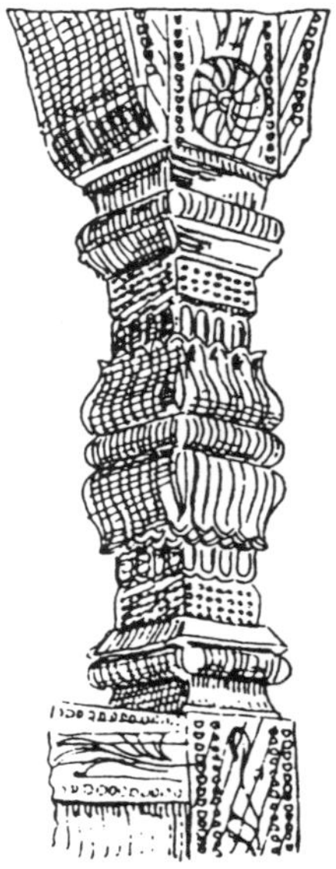

EASTERN EUROPEAN PATTERN AND ARCHITECTURE

Motifs, patterns and architectural details from Poland, Croatia and Russia dating from the 16th to 18th centuries: their styles display a mixture of influences, from the Italian Renaissance and from the Orient, the latter especially true of Russia. The resultant indigenous traditions are complex. Many buildings of this period are wooden: details from a Croatian peasant's house *top and centre left*. A window *opposite top* from the Royal Castle, Cracow, carved in stone, displays stronger Italian influence while the 17thC bishop's mitre from the Kremlin *opposite centre* has a Byzantine character, as befits the Orthodox faith.

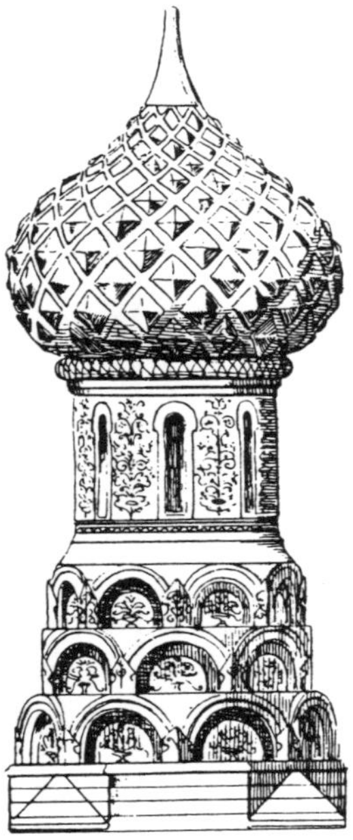

RUSSIAN DECORATION

An indigenous Russian style of decoration emerged in the 12th and 13th centuries, which in turn absorbed Byzantine influences from Greek and Lombard artists and craftsmen, imported into Russia. The Tartar regime (1237–1480) added Mongol influences. Characteristic Russian architectural forms include the onion dome and ogival arch, both seen on *this page.*

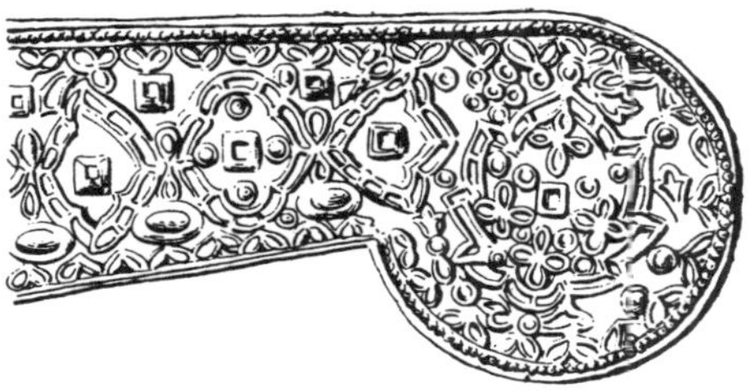

RUSSIAN MANUSCRIPT ILLUMINATION

Further differing styles of Russian ornament can be seen in Slavo-Russian illuminated manuscripts from St Petersburg. Those on *this page,* from engravings by Nicolas Vassilief, show Russian interpretations of strapwork. The examples *opposite* show Russian adaptations of Celtic interlace pattern. They are from manuscripts in the former Imperial Library, St Petersburg.

RUSSIAN MANUSCRIPT MOTIFS

Motifs taken from a selection of Russian illuminated manuscripts dating from the 15th to 17th centuries formerly in the Imperial Public Library, St Petersburg. They form part of a collection originally researched and compiled by Vladimir Stassov, first published in St Petersburg in 1887. Many of the manuscripts' original locations no longer exist but this anthology represents an indication of the wide range of styles used.

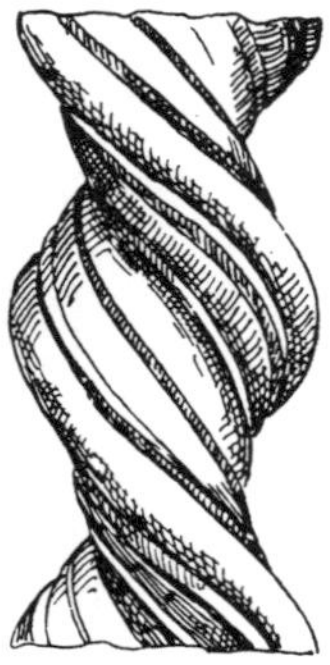

ITALIAN RENAISSANCE ARCHITECTURAL ORNAMENT

Techniques illustrated include sgraffito (incised plasterwork) *this page upper right* and *opposite centre and bottom centre. Opposite left* details of the principal facade, Certosa of Pavia (begun 1473). *Opposite top right* detail from Raphael's paintings in the Loggie, the Vatican, Rome. *Opposite top centre* coat of arms from the Palazzo Vecchio, Florence.

RENAISSANCE ARCHITECTURAL DETAILS

This page stone brackets from buildings in Pisa *top* and Florence *above* illustrate the decorative use of classically inspired ornament, including egg-and-dart moulding *above left* and acanthus leaves. *Opposite left, t–b* detail from the stalls, San Pietro; cresting from the roof of the Louvre, Paris; Cathedral stall cresting, Perugia; cresting from the stalls, San Pietro. *Opposite top right* bracket from a crest in the Town Hall, Perugia. These show the use of a winged lion, satyr's head, rams' heads and eagles, all inspired by classical prototypes.

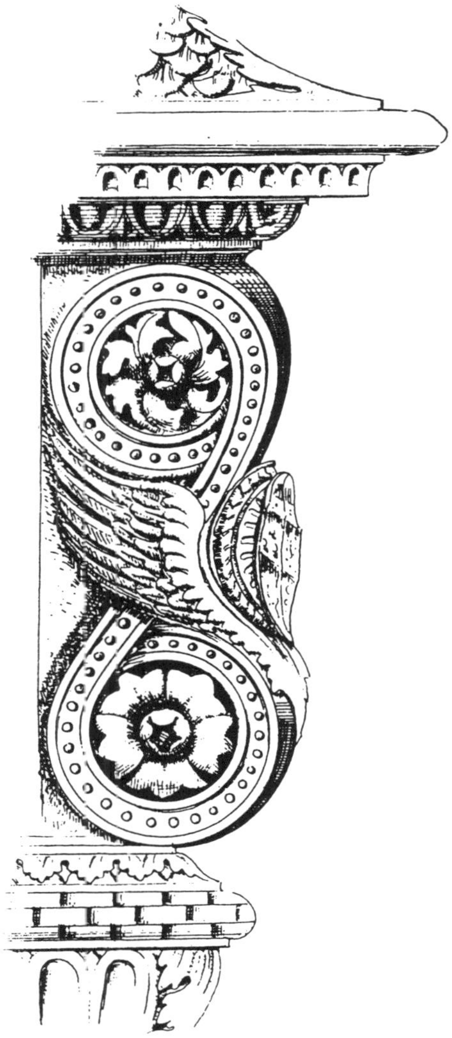

RENAISSANCE ORNAMENT

Engraved ivories *this page* include details of an ebony cabinet *left and right,* based on Raphael's paintings in the Vatican Loggie; a panel *centre* from a chair formerly in the collection of M. Bonlay de la Meurthe, based on an engraving in the Vatican Library; and *above* a panel based on a design by Agostino of Venice. *Opposite* are 16thC frescoes and arabesques by Raphael, from the Vatican Loggie.

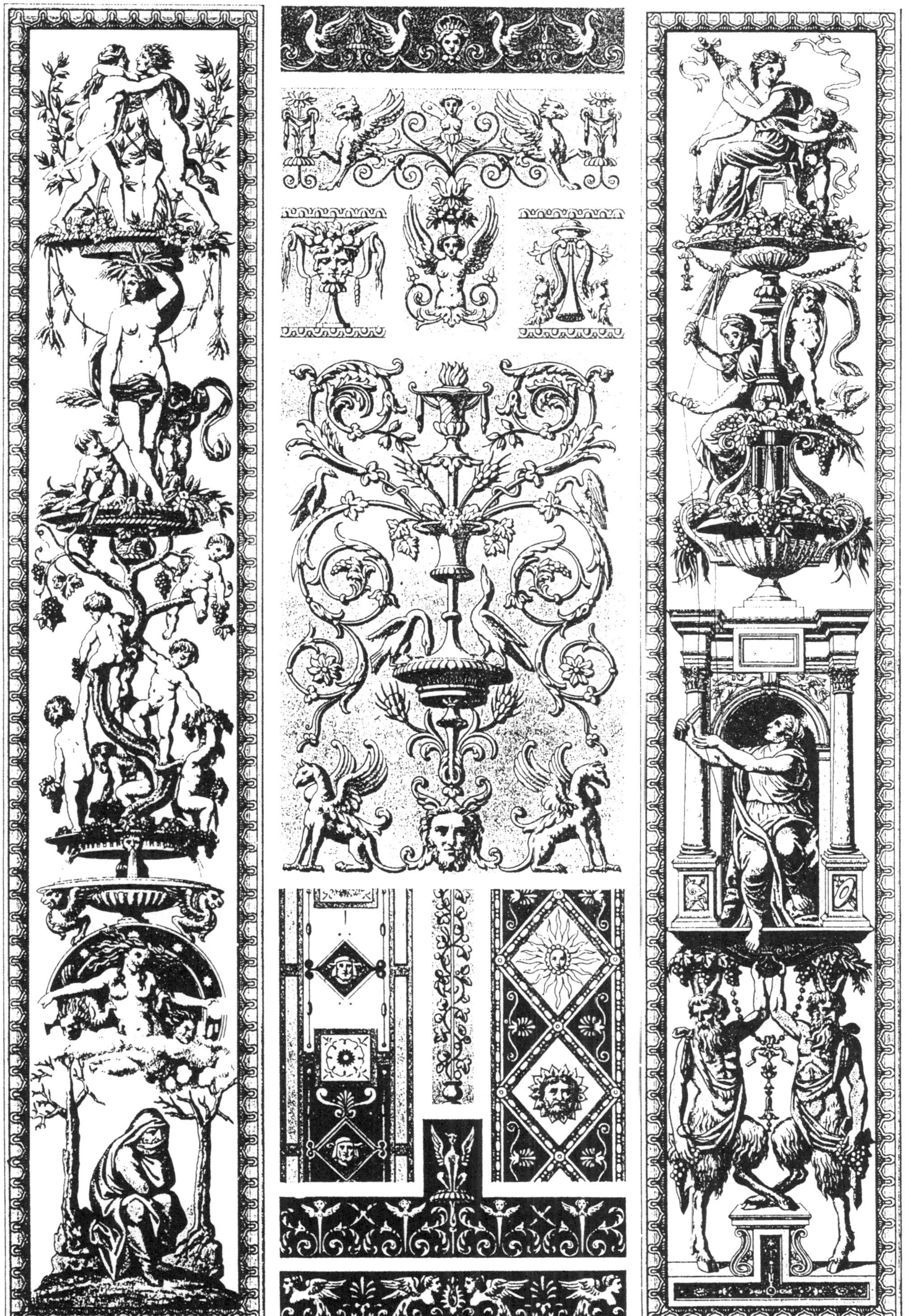

RENAISSANCE BORDERS AND PANELS

This page, l–r soffit panel from one of the Genoese palaces; detail of a small pilaster showing the springing of scroll-work, by the Lombardi, in the Church of Sta Maria dei Miracoli, Venice; detail from the Gate of the Baptistery, Florence; arabesque designed by Baccio Pintelli, Church of St Agostino, Rome. *Opposite* are border panels from 15th and 16thC illuminated manuscripts. Panels 2–6 *centre top* are wide and narrow margins from the Prayers to the Virgin Mary manuscript made for Alessandro de Medici, first Duke of Florence (d. 1537), a few months after his marriage to Margaret, illegitimate daughter of Charles V of Spain. These portraits face one another.

EN TOVT HONNE
REDOVBTE

ITALIAN RENAISSANCE ORNAMENT

This page 14th – 16thC graphic art, including book illustration, a book marker *top left,* and designs for embroidery *top centre* (Venetian, 1529). Textile and costume designs include *top right* 16thC silk damask. *Above left* is a 16thC headdress. *Centre right* is a detail from the marble floor mosaic of Siena Cathedral by Beccafumi (dated 1372). *Opposite* is an example of intarsia work from a stall in the church of Sta Maria Novella, Florence *top left;* and *right, t–b* a 16thC coffer and table; and a bronze knocker (Strozzi Palace, Florence). The lower four images are examples of majolica (tin-glazed earthenware pottery) from Siena, Urbino, Gubbio and Cafaggiolo.

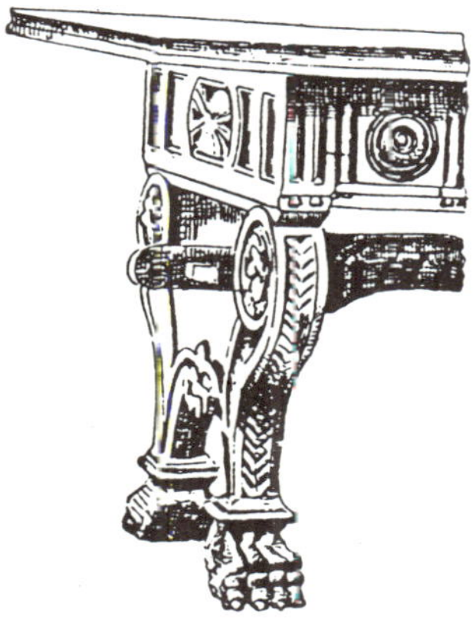

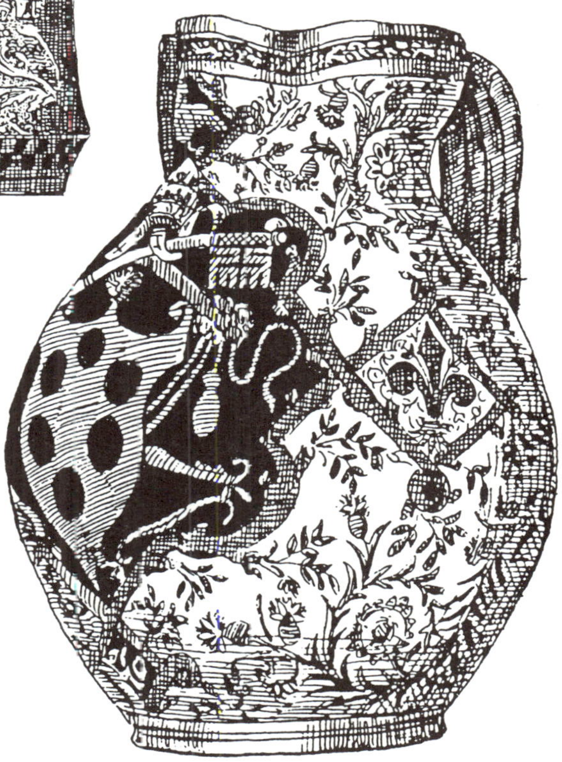

FRENCH RENAISSANCE ORNAMENT

Details shown include a capital from the Porte Dauphine at Fontainebleau *above left,* and pilasters from the Chapel of St Saturin and the Baptistery of Louis XIII. The ceremonial helmet was made for the French king Charles the Bold, set with pearls and precious stones. *Opposite* examples of outstanding craftsmanship include samples of Valenciennes lace *top right,* an embroidered bed hanging presented to the Trappists near Montaigne by Henri II, a book cover bearing his arms *bottom left.* The hand mirror was designed by Etienne de Laune, and the key, dating from 1625, is by Mathurin Jousse de la Flèche.

FRENCH RENAISSANCE AND ROCOCO ORNAMENT

Illustrations include *left and right* carved oak panels in the Louvre, Paris, c1520; *above and top centre* carved door panels from the Château d'Anet (now at the Ecole des Beaux Arts, Paris), 1548. *Opposite left* is a panel of carved ornament from the Château de Gaillon, c1505; *centre* are three pilasters from the Monument to Louis XII, St Denis, c1520; *right* is a detail of a carved wooden panel from the cathedral of Notre Dame, Paris, in the French Rococo Louis Quinze style, showing the use of the conch shell motif. *Below* is a detail of a chimneypiece in the Louvre, designed by Germaine Pilon.

SPANISH RENAISSANCE ORNAMENT

Illustrations include *this page, top row, l–r* iron railing, Siguenza cathedral; bracket capital, Archiepiscopal Palace, Alcalá de Henares; inner gallery, Polentina House, Avila. *Middle row, l–r* corner piece of the tomb of Cardinal Ximenez, Alcalá de Henares; gateway, Avila. *Opposite, top left and right* figures from the facade of the University in Alcalá de Henares; *centre right* folding chair, Toledo Cathedral; *bottom left* 16thC secretaire; *centre* helmet from the Armeria, Madrid.

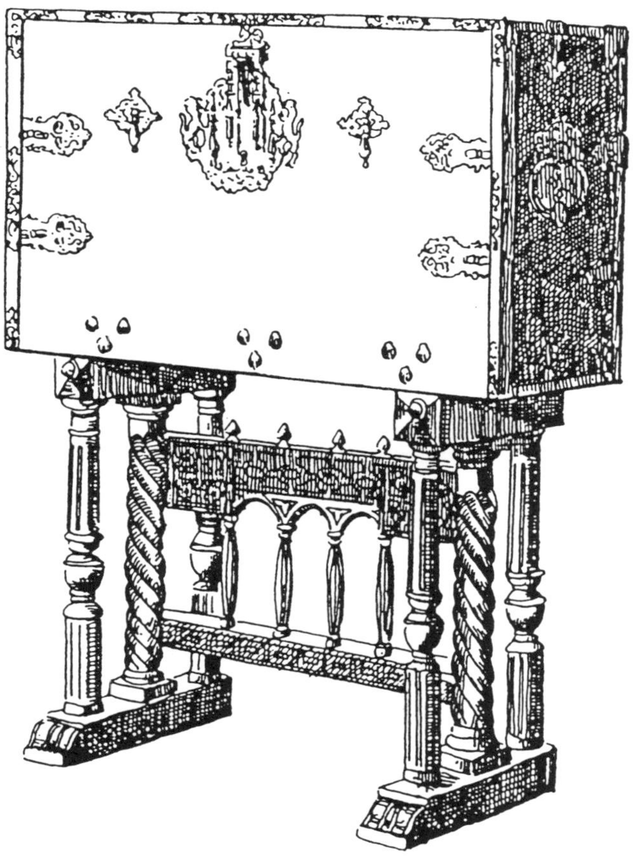

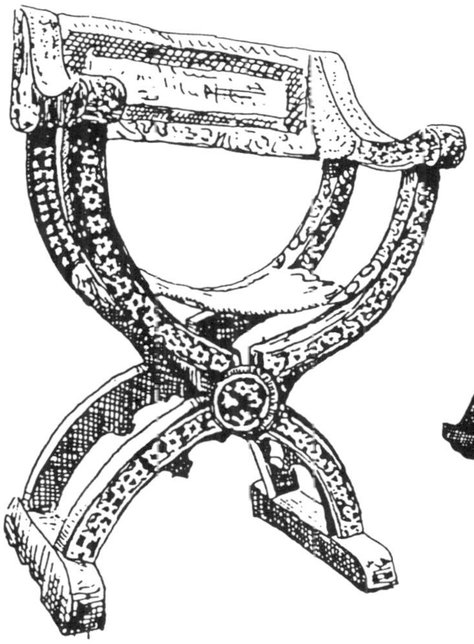

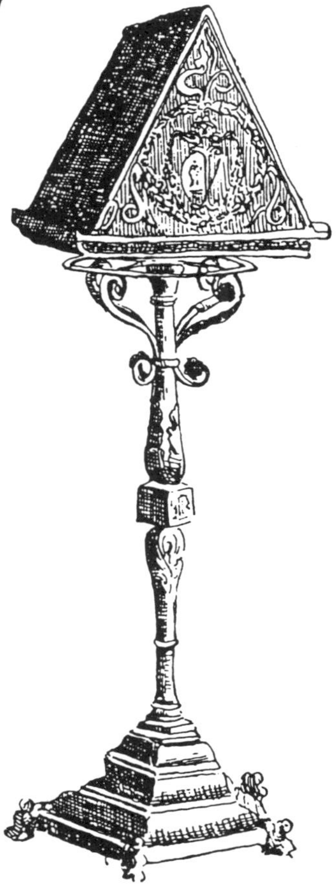

GERMAN AND SWISS RENAISSANCE ORNAMENT

Top left incised stone 'Solnhofer' slab, 1592 (Historical Society of the Oberpfalz in Ratisbon). *Above, l–r* silver gilt tankard made in Nuremberg, 16th or early 17thC; silver gilt wedding goblet, 18thC; 17thC hock glass (National Museum, Munich). *Right* detail of panelling from the granary, Langnau, Canton Berne, Switzerland, dating from 1519, showing a local adaptation of Renaissance architectural ornament.

GERMAN IRONWORK

Examples of German Renaissance ironwork. *Top left* gate from the Church of St Ulrich, Augsburg. *Top right* section of wrought iron screen, Fuggers Chapel. Church of St Ulrich, Augsburg. *Above* iron hinge, Ulm Cathedral.

NORTHERN RENAISSANCE: BELGIUM, HOLLAND AND SCANDINAVIA

The influence of the Renaissance spread north, through Belgium from 1520, to Holland, and from there to northern Germany and Scandinavia. Its impact in Norway was not felt until the 17th century. Note the Delft plates *opposite bottom left,* Norwegian woodwork *opposite centre left,* and also the use of strapwork for hinges and atlantes (male support figures). These are shown on the Dutch cabinet *opposite top right.* Note also the term (tapering pedestal or support) with a human head *this page top right,* a detail of a stall in the Stadtor of Dordrecht.

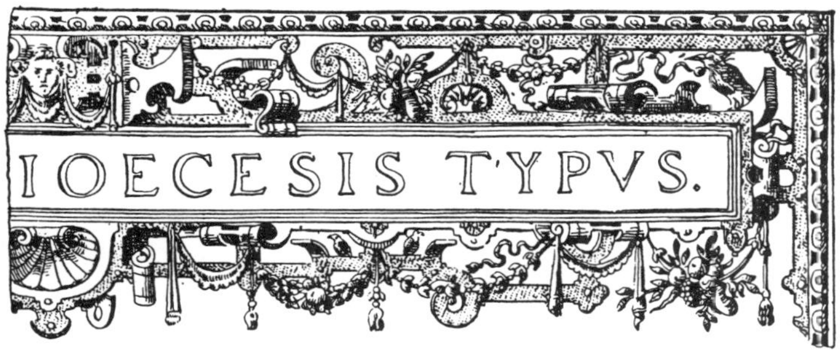
IOECESIS TYPVS.

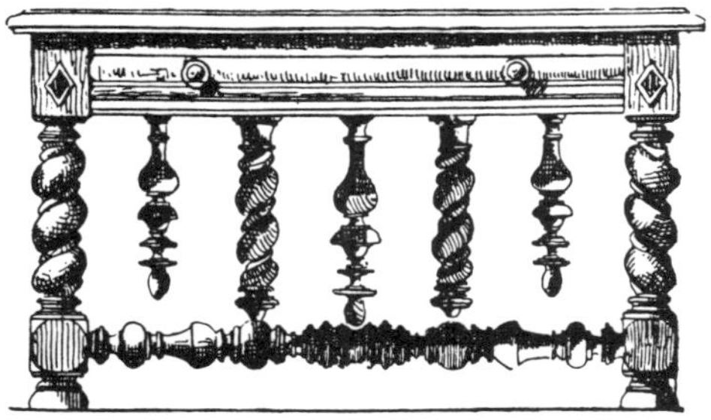

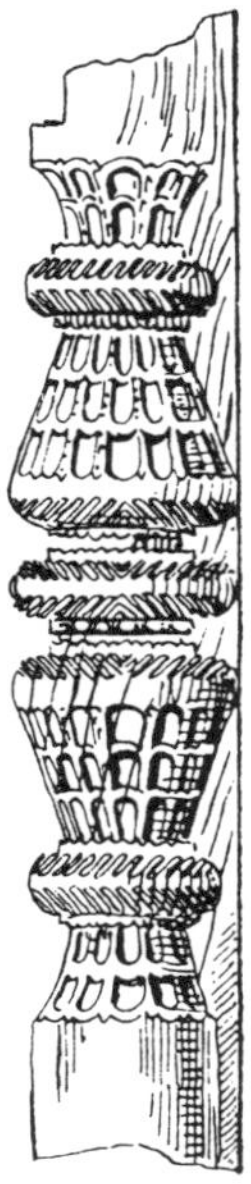

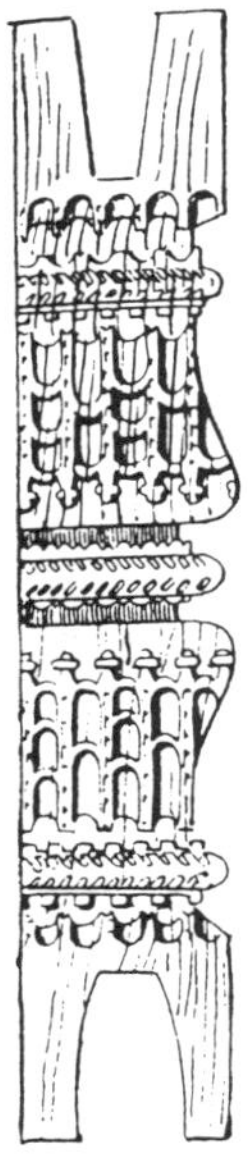

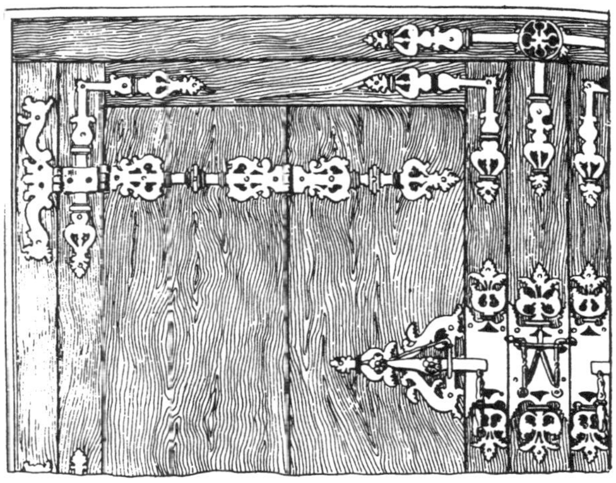

ENGLISH RENAISSANCE DECORATION: ELIZABETHAN AND EARLY STUART

Between 1558 and 1649 English Renaissance design and decoration drew inspiration and influence from Italian, French, German and Dutch sources, both through the influx of foreign designers and craftsmen, and via pattern books, for example, by Vredeman de Vries. Characteristics include the use of strapwork in ornament, and furniture made of oak. Fully upholstered chairs are introduced: *opposite top right* is a 17thC chair from Hampton Court with figured velvet upholstery. The two textile designs *opposite bottom right* are both for appliqué embroidery, and date from the early 17th century.

6

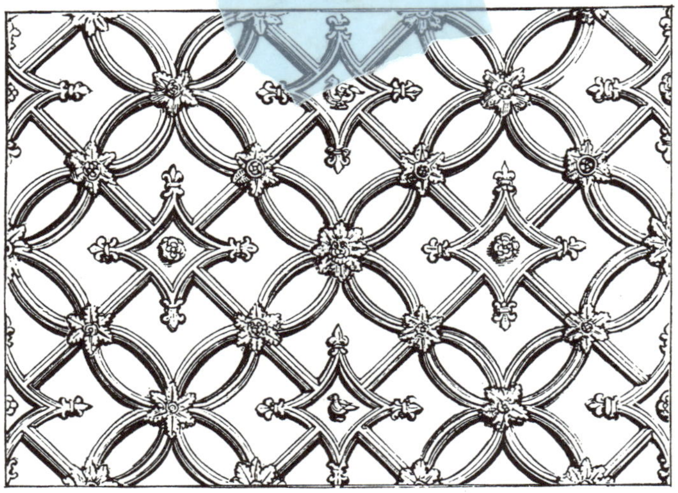

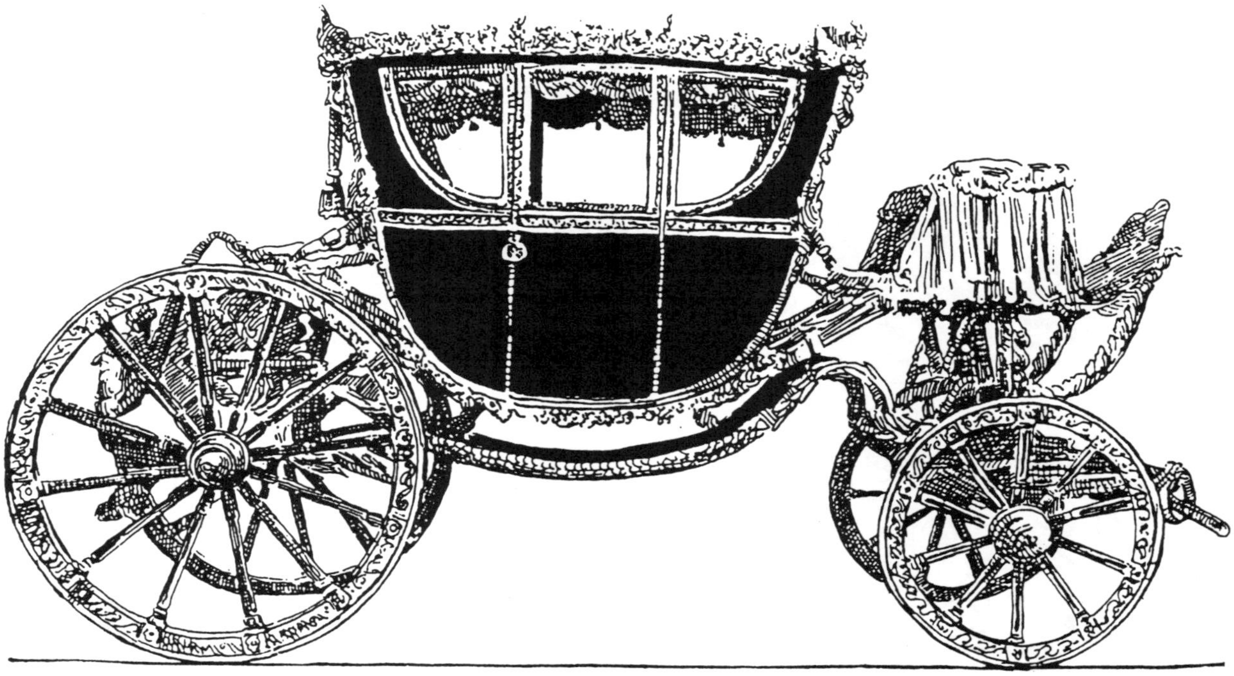

ITALIAN LATER RENAISSANCE ORNAMENT

The transition from the Renaissance to the Baroque movements in art, architecture and design occurred in Italy between the late 16th and early 17th centuries. The style of ornament is more florid and elaborate during the early Baroque period, in turn evolving into the lightness and grace of the Rococo style in the early 18th century. Illustrations include *top left* the wheel of a state carriage designed by Filippe Passarini (b. Rome 1638), and *centre right* the cresting of a cupboard in the Parma Museum. The two lamps *opposite top left and right* are both 17thC, and in the collection of the Kunstgewerbe Museum, Berlin. The textiles shown are examples of 17thC Venetian lace collars, a gold embroidered table cover *opposite bottom left,* Genoese silk velvet *opposite bottom centre* and a Genoese panel, embroidered in silk on a gold ground.

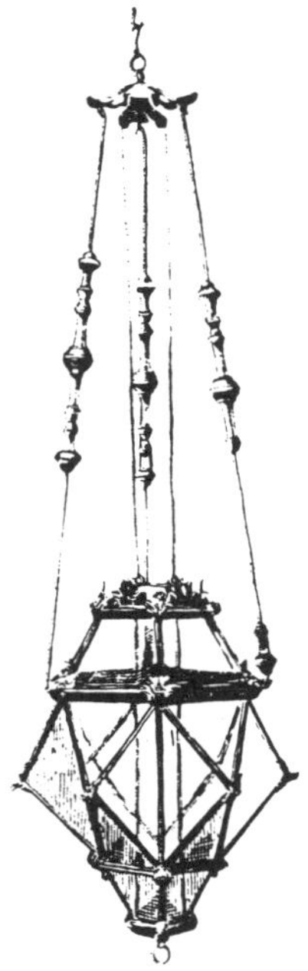

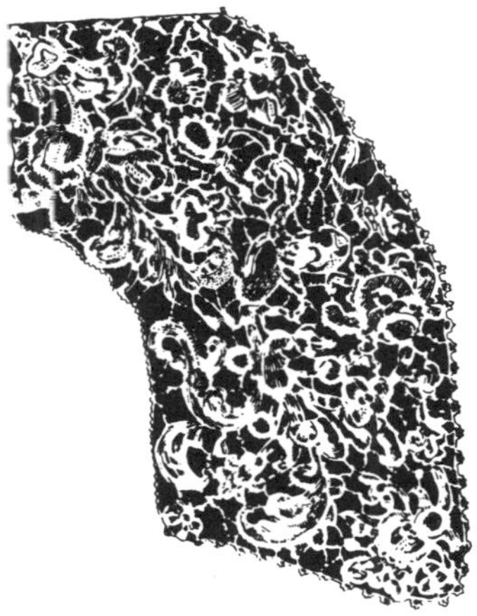

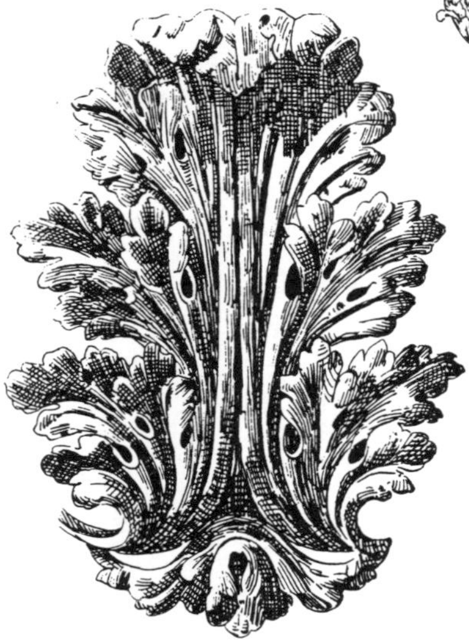

FRENCH BAROQUE ORNAMENT

Top, l–r handle of a vase by Anton Coyzevox (active in Paris 1640–1720); acanthus leaf; vase in the park at Versailles. *Above, l–r* mural decoration after Berain; ceiling decoration after Daniel Marot (1640–1712); design for mural decoration by Gilles Oppenport. Illustrations *opposite* include ornaments for rifle mountings, designs for a gate and for locksmith's plates by Hugh Brisville, from designs by Berain. *Bottom left* is a console for a mantelpiece, in chased, gilt bronze; *bottom right* a curtain design by Daniel Marot.

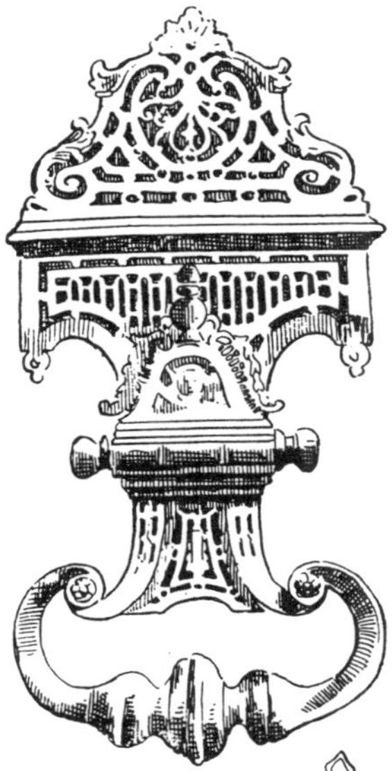

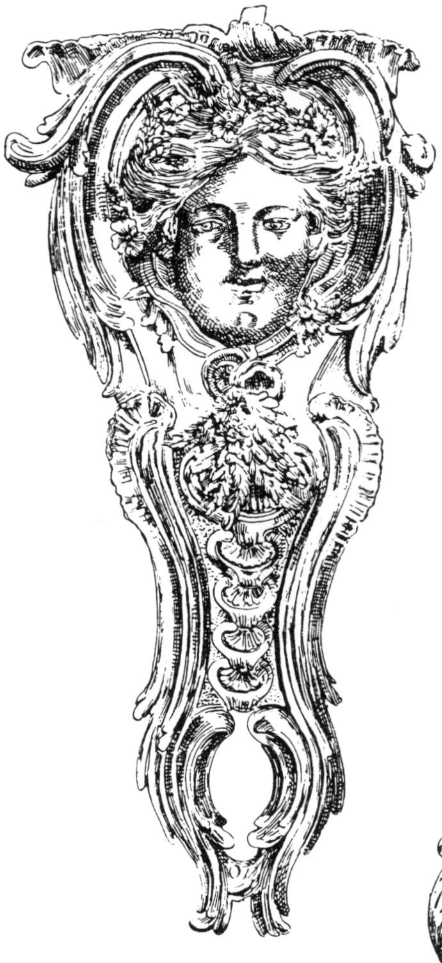
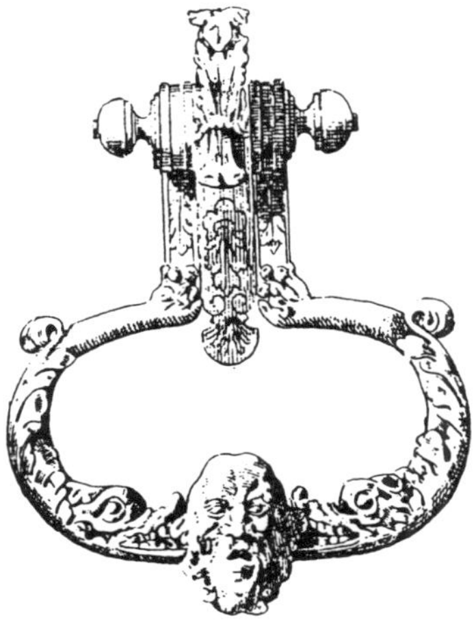

FRENCH BAROQUE AND ROCOCO ORNAMENT

Top are designs for Rococo wood carving, including trophies of arms by Girardon from Versailles; and a sword scabbard; *above* are examples of 16th and 17thC Baroque goldsmithing. *Opposite* are 17thC mural paintings, miniatures, enamels and engravings in niello, including *top* part of the painted ceiling in the apartment of Anne of Austria in the Palace of the Louvre, and *bottom left and right* panels from the Queen Mother's pavilion at Fontainebleau and from the Luxembourg Palace.

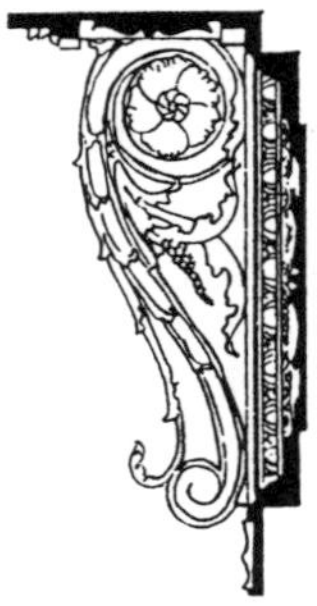

ENGLISH BAROQUE ARCHITECTURAL ORNAMENT

Top left fireplace in the Salon at Forde Abbey, Dorset. *Top right* organ case, St Mary Woolnorth, London. *Above* sundial from Wrest, Bedfordshire; *above right* Soffit from the Gallery of the Senate House, Cambridge and *below* detail of stall end, St Paul's Cathedral. *Opposite* are examples of carved and cast architectural ornament in plaster, wood and stone. Sources include Clifford's Inn, the church of St Mary Woolnorth, St Paul's Cathedral, London, and the Senate House, Cambridge.

FRENCH ROCOCO ORNAMENT

Decorative carvings from the private apartments of Louis XV at Versailles. The work dates from c1750, and is attributed to Verberckt. *Opposite* are designs for tapestries by Gillot, commissioned for weaving at the Gobelins workshops in Paris. The chair back, *top centre* represents La Fontaine's Fable of the Oak and the Reed.

ROCOCO DESIGN

Above is a selection of designs for woven silks, of the types produced in Lyon in the late 18th century. The patterns range from designs suitable for wall coverings and curtains to finer, smaller-striped designs, intended for clothing. The undulating ribbon 'S' stripes are typical of Lyon silks. *Opposite* is a design for interior decoration by Franz Xavier Habermann (1721–96). A German teacher of perspective and architectural drawing, Habermann published over 500 prints after 1781.

CHINOISERIE

Designs for Chinese-style railings and gates, dating from the mid 18th century. Combining rectilinear precision with decorative grace, Chinese-style fretwork was highly popular in the 18th century. *Opposite* is a selection of mid 18thC Chinoiserie designs for china cabinets, by Thomas Chippendale (1718–79), first published by him in 1754 in The Gentleman and Cabinet-Maker's Director.

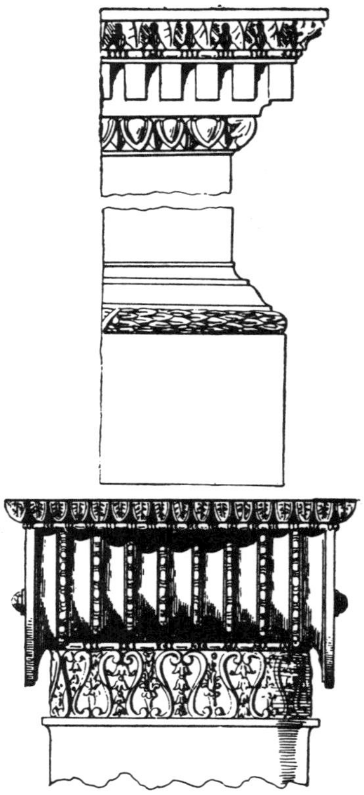

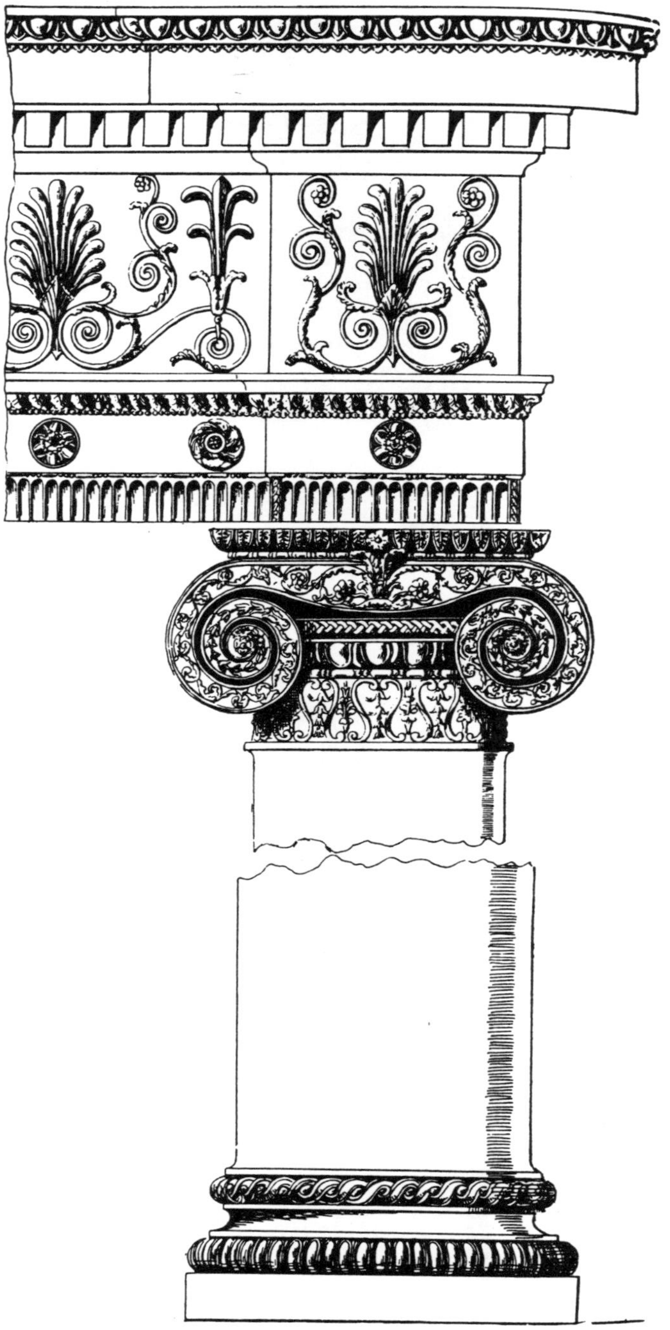

NEOCLASSICAL DESIGN

Top details of designs by Robert Adam for the entrance hall of Shelburne House, Berkeley Square, London. *Above right* column and entablature at Syon House, Middlesex, also designed by Robert Adam. *Above left* doorway from Syon House. *Opposite* further details from Syon House, including the moulding round the bas-reliefs in the hall, and a vase on the porter's lodge. *Right* Greek order entablature, capital and pilaster from the dining room of a house originally designed by Robert Adam for Sir Watkins Williams Wynn, in London.

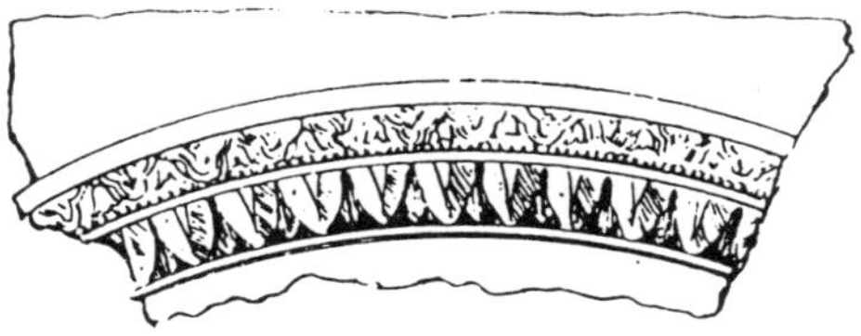

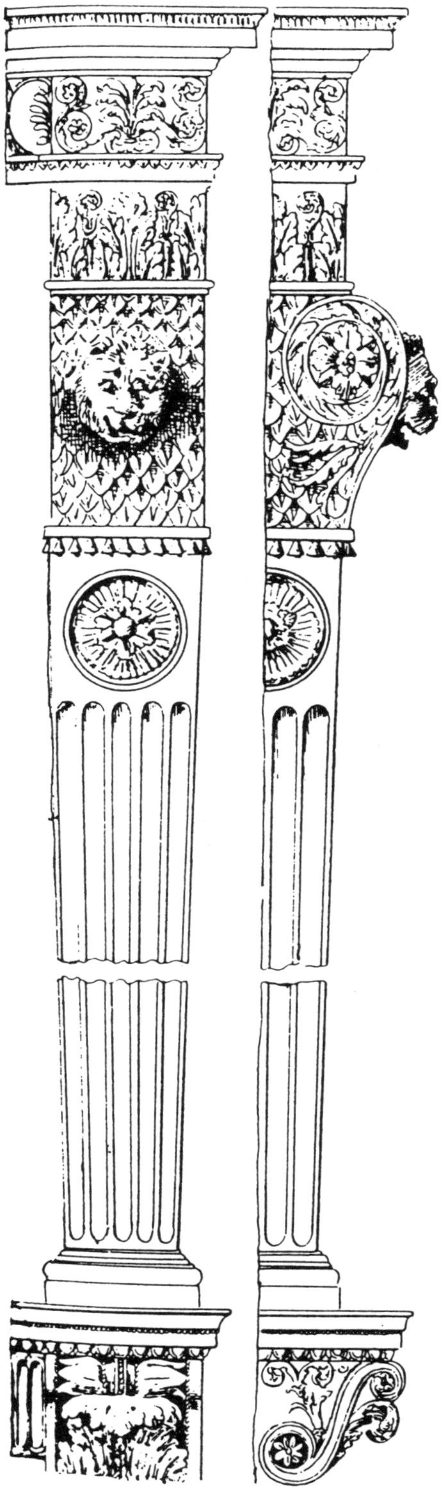

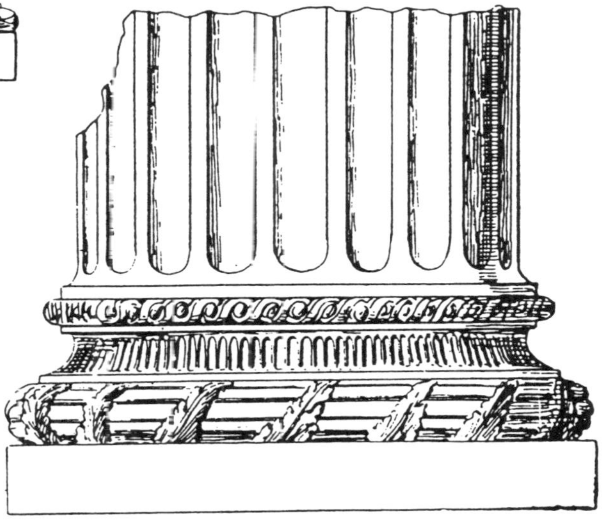

NEOCLASSICAL DESIGN

Top left panel designed by Pergolesi; *above centre right* design by Robert Adam for the ceiling of the music room in the house of Sir Watkins Williams Wynn; *above right* a window mantle and *above left* the top of a chest of drawers also by Adam. *Opposite* are details of ceiling designs by Adam; a table centrepiece *bottom;* mantelpiece designs *centre right* by G. Richardson and W. Thomas; and the lid of a piano *centre left* in wood of various colours, designed by Adam and made in London for the Empress of Russia.

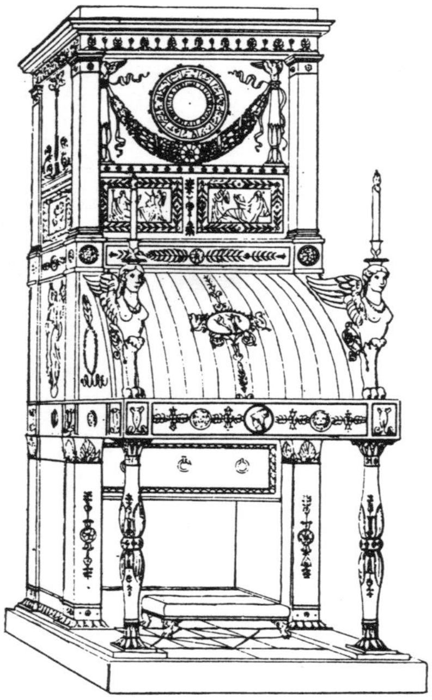

FRENCH EMPIRE ORNAMENT

The patronage of Napoleon stimulated a classical revival in architecture, art and design, evident in details from the Venus Museum in the Louvre *left,* the Hall of the Marshalls in the Tuileries *centre,* and in French Empire furniture and decorative furniture mountings *right.*

French Empire furniture and design is noted for its sense of elegance and luxury within a classical vocabulary. The (now destroyed) throne of Napoleon I *above* in the Tuileries, designed by Percier & Fontaine, uses his characteristic bee motif for its draped fabric hangings.

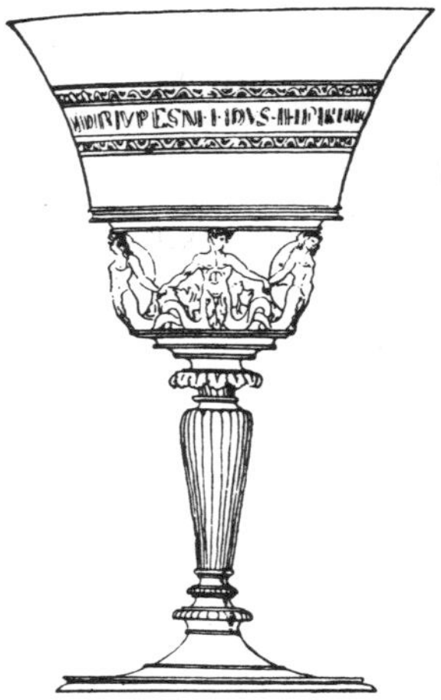

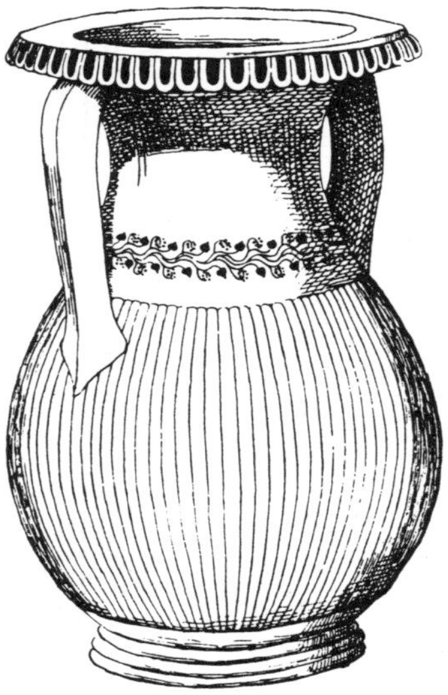

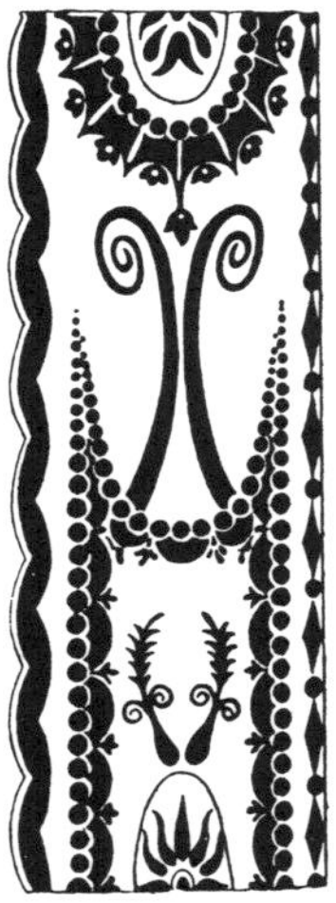

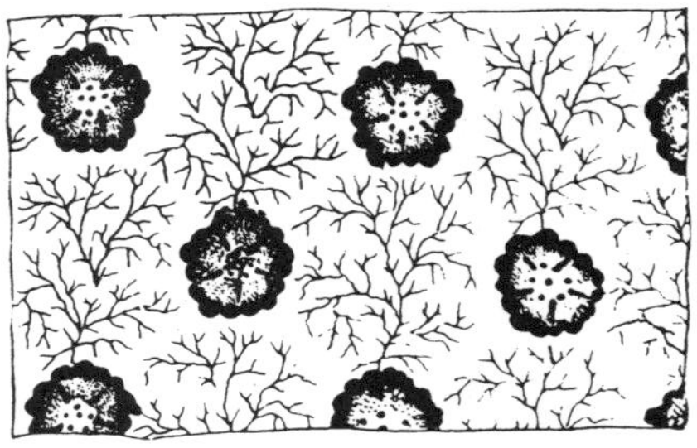

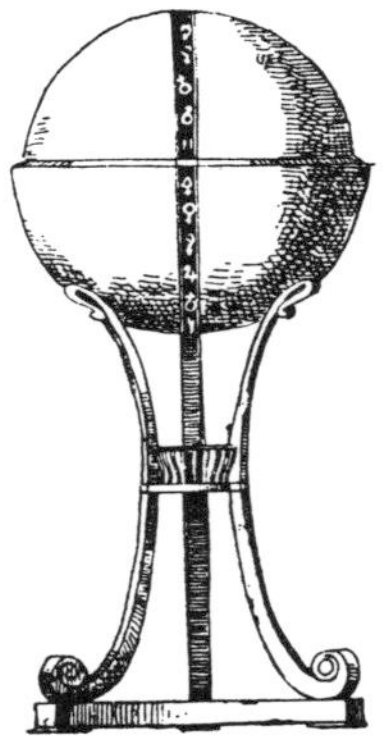

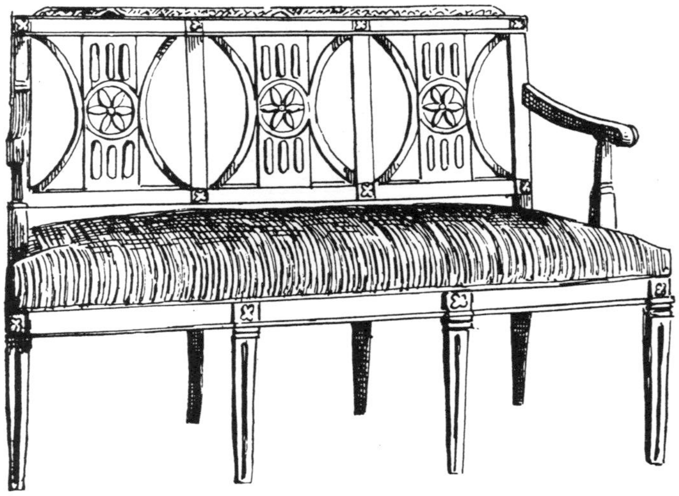

GERMAN BIEDERMEIER AND NEO-GREC DESIGN 1815–1848

'Biedermeier' is the term given to early 19thC German design and decoration in the classical manner; furniture features fruitwoods and mahogany, and painted details in black and gold. In the 1830s and 1840s, the architects Schinkel and Klenze led a stricter revival of Greek classical design, referred to as 'Neo-Grec'.

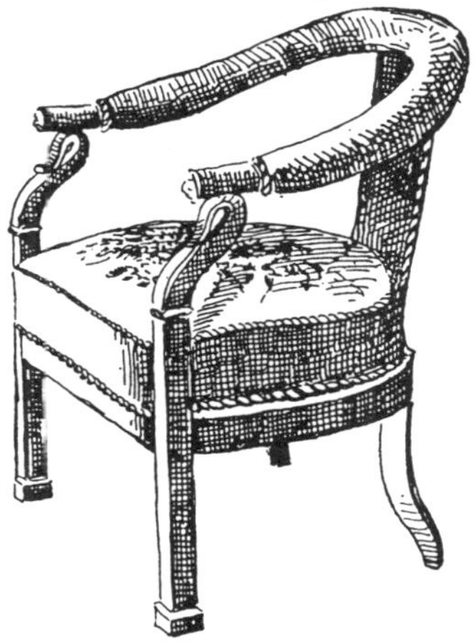

THE GOTHIC REVIVAL

The 19thC phase of the Gothic Revival sought to recreate the principles and practices of medieval Gothic architecture and design. To fulfil the popular thirst for Gothic style imagery, the designer John Leighton produced an anthology of designs in the Gothic manner, from which this selection is drawn.

THE RENAISSANCE REVIVAL

A further selection of designs by John Leighton, this time in the Renaissance manner, demonstrate the eclecticism which dominated mid 19thC architecture and design. An interest in the grotesque and a heavy style of engraving are two of the differences between these designs and their Renaissance prototypes.

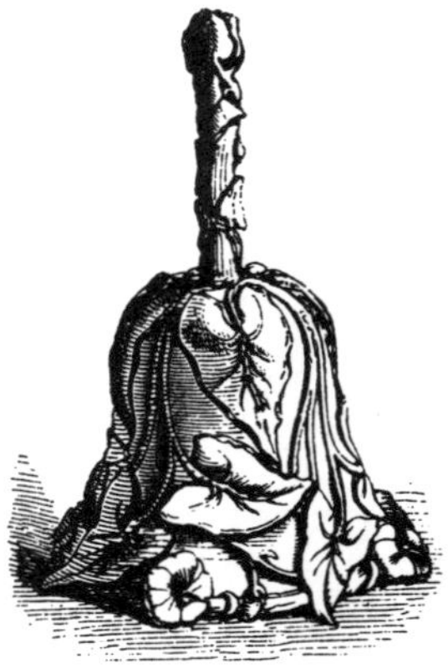

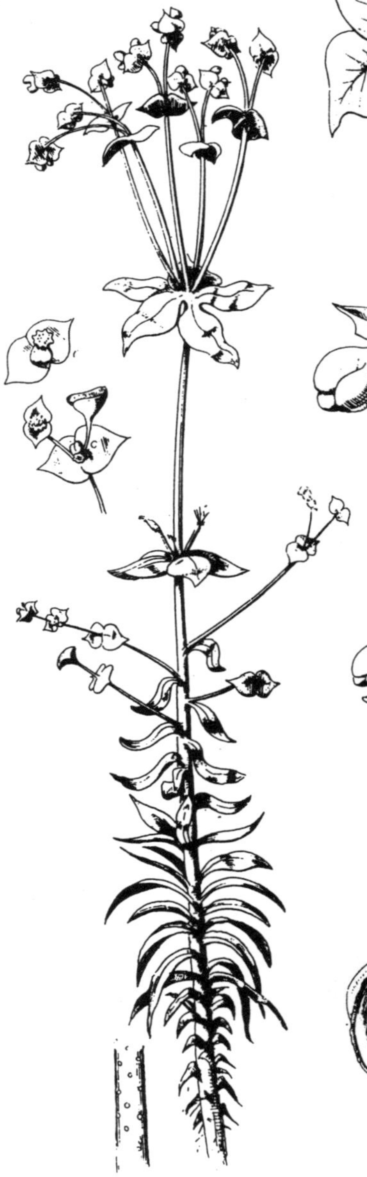

NATURALISM

From the 1850s, prompted by pattern books such as The Grammar of Ornament (1856) by the designer and theorist Owen Jones, designers sought renewed inspiration in nature. Shown both naturalistically and schematized, plants and flowers were especially popular.

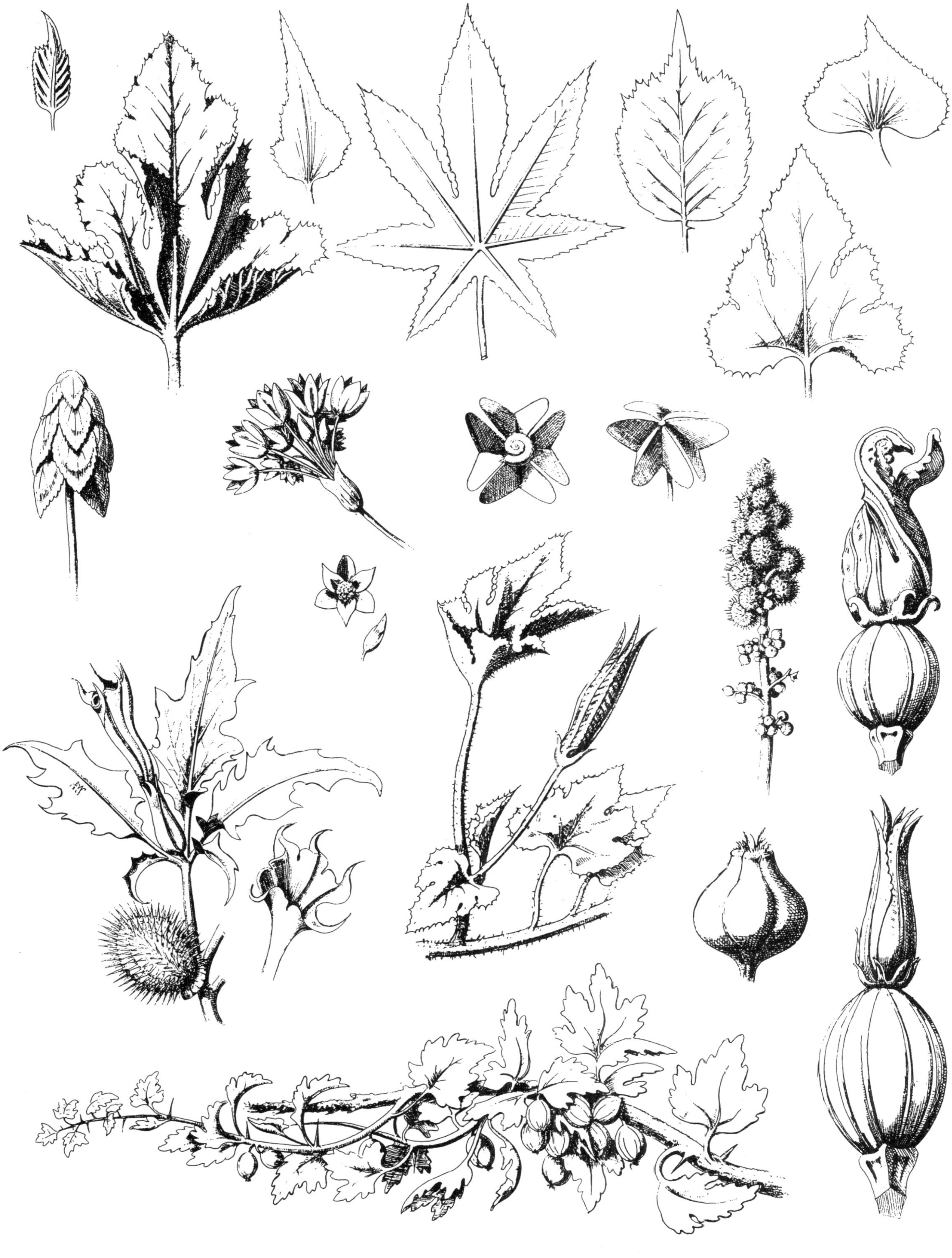

CHRISTOPHER DRESSER AND THE AESTHETIC MOVEMENT

Dr Christopher Dresser (1834–1904) was a prominent English botanist, design theorist and designer of silver holloware, cast iron, glass and ceramics. His graphic work, of which a selection is illustrated here, occupies a transitional role between the formal stylization of the Gothic Revival and the linear abstraction and sinuous curves of Art Nouveau, and also shows the influence of his study tour of Japan in 1876–7.

ART NOUVEAU BOOK BINDINGS AND BOOK-PLATES

During the 1890s, Art Nouveau became internationally popular as a style in art, architecture and design. Periodicals and art magazines such as The Studio in England and Ver Sacrum in Germany promoted the new style; this selection of book bindings and book-plates was published in The Studio. The 'Ex Libris' book-plates were winning designs in one of its many competitions to find new talent.

EX·LIBRIS
CHARLES
STEWART
KING

EX LIBRIS
P·C·KONODY

ex·libris
hugh·giffen
Mc·kinney·

EX LIBRIS
KATE PEMBURY

SIR
EDWARD
BURNE·
JONES
A RECORD
& REVIEW
BY
MALCOLM
BELL
G.BELL & SONS.

SIR EDWARD
BURNE-JONES
A RECORD AND
REVIEW

EX·LIBRIS:
CISSIE·ALLSOPP:

ART NOUVEAU GRAPHICS

A selection of decorative end-pieces and illuminated letters published in The Studio.

ART NOUVEAU BOOK-PLATES

A further selection of Art Nouveau graphics. Styles of 1890s book illustration vary from near abstraction, as in the illustrations *top left and right,* based on images of can-can dancers, to designs which are still strongly rooted in historicist idioms, as in the proposed book-plates for William Snelling Hadway.

Ex libris
William
Snelling Hadaway

EX LIBRIS
Simon Peter said, I go a fishing: and they said, We also wil go with thee.
LOUIS RHEAD

EX LIBRIS
·W·H·SHIR-CLIFF·
18·WASHINGTON·97

EX LIBRIS
CHARLES DYER
MILWAUKEE

ART NOUVEAU BOOK ILLUSTRATION

A selection of German book plates and illustrations. The narrow strips of animal illustrations above are especially remarkable for their effective use of very confined spaces.

ASIA

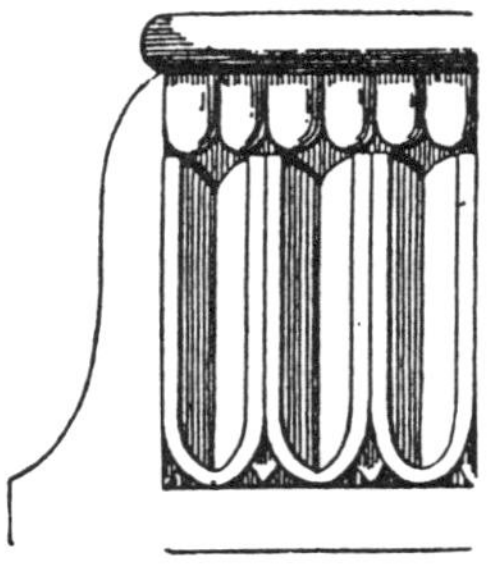

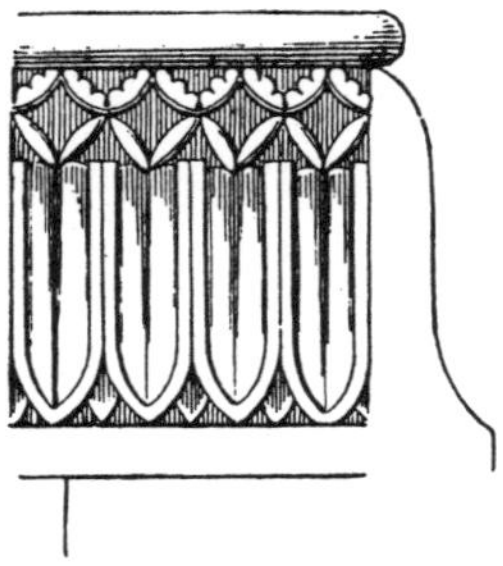

ASSYRIAN ORNAMENT

Between c2000 and 603 BC, the kingdom of Assyria dominated Western Asia. Ornament such as the griffon brick relief *above centre* was used extensively on Assyrian brick buildings. Note also the popularity of the lotus leaf and flower *opposite top centre and bottom left.*

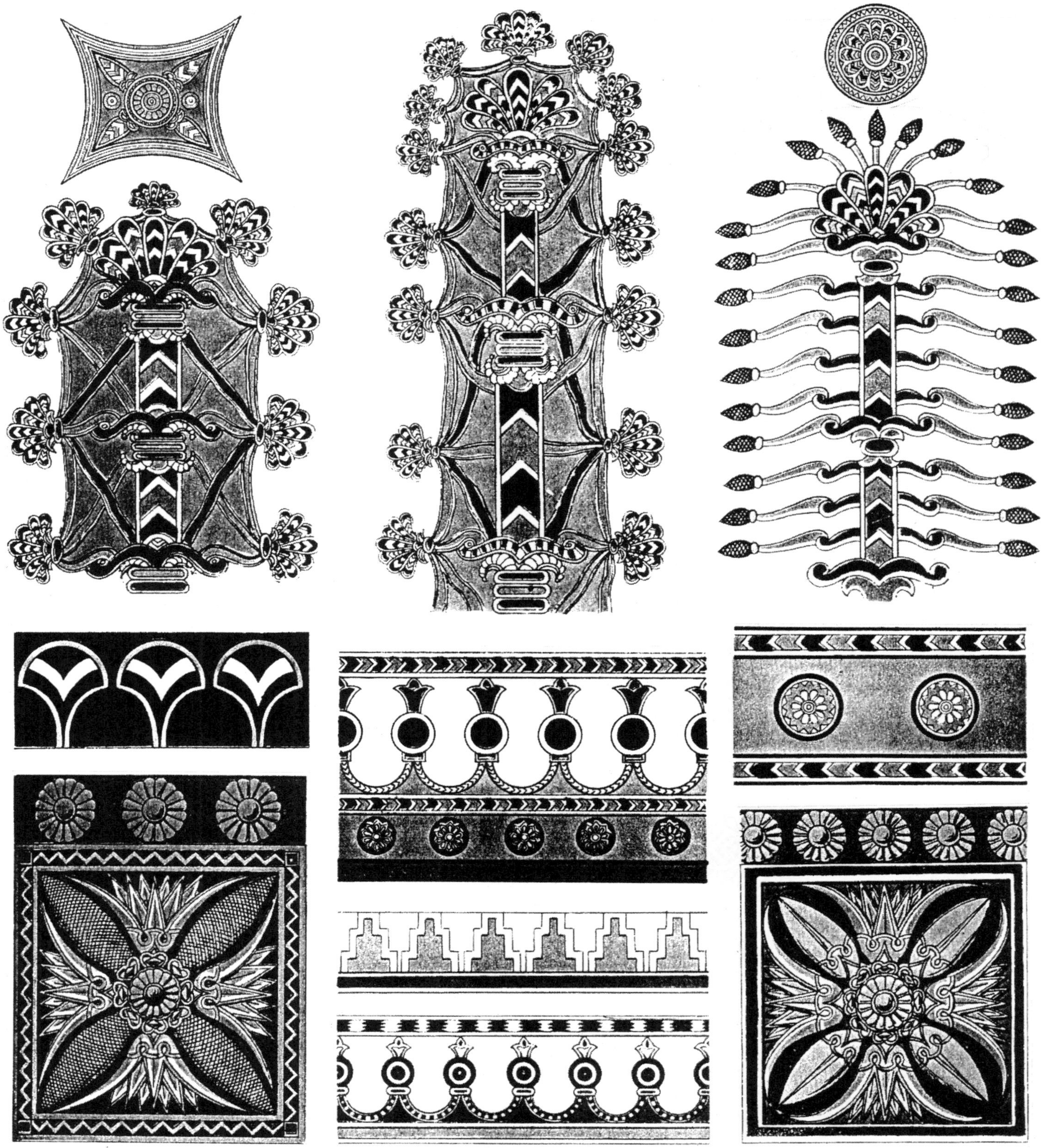

ASSYRIAN ORNAMENT

Top three sacred trees from Nimrud; *above* details of sculptured pavements from Kouyunjik and painted ornaments from Nimrud, all excavated and originally published by A. H. Layard. Assyrian ornament seems strongly influenced by Egyptian art, on which it was closely modelled.

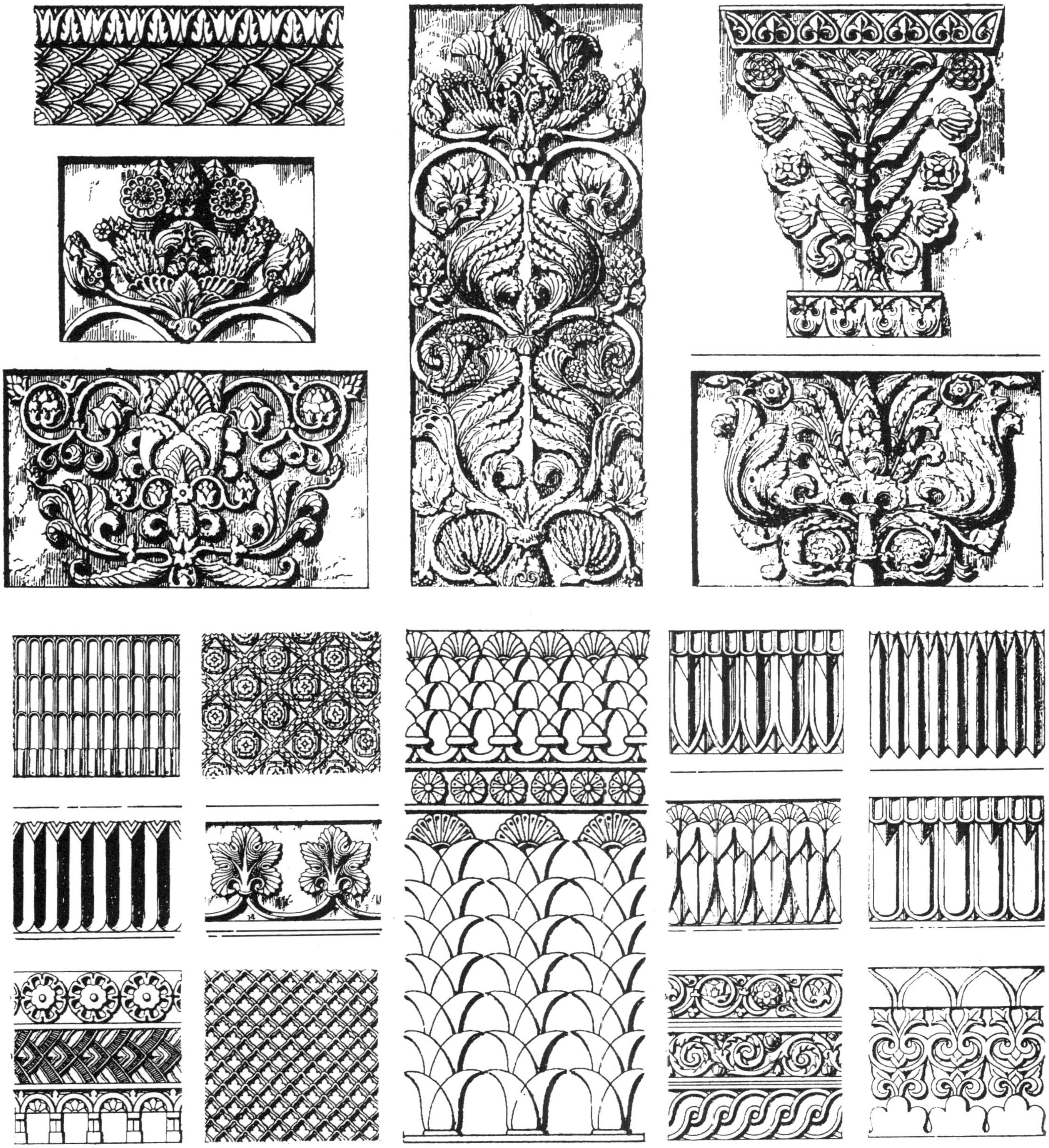

PERSIAN ORNAMENT

Sassanian Persian motifs taken from sites at Persepolis, Tak i Bostan and Ispahan. Buildings constructed under the Sassanian dynasty (226 BC – AD 642) were of brick and decorated with carved stucco. The low-relief capitals from pilasters and the panel *centre* show the influence of Roman sculpture. The lozenge-shaped diaper pattern *bottom right* is the first historical use of this form.

ASSYRIAN AND PERSIAN ORNAMENT

Sources for this range of highly stylized motifs and decorative patterns include glazed bricks, low-relief carved friezes and metalware.

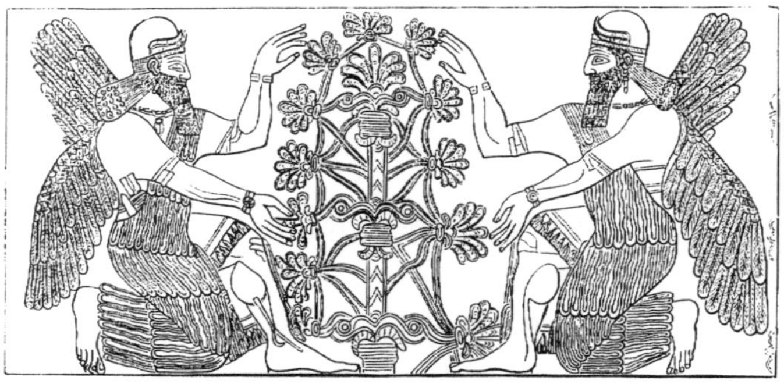

PERSIAN ORNAMENT

This page shows architectural details, glazed tile panels and ceramics from Ispahan, and *right* a tile panel from a palace of Shah Abbas the Great. *Opposite* is a selection of motifs in the Islamic manner, compiled by John Leighton in the 19th century. Note the peacock *centre*, the Persian imperial symbol.

PERSIAN TILE PANELS

A selection of Persian designs, dating from the 16th and 17th centuries; originally for glazed internal tile panels, these are also suitable for carpets, textiles and decorative borders. The Koran forbade the representation of the human figure.

PERSIAN AND ARABIC ORNAMENT

Persian tin and copper work, decorated with gems, gilded and silvered, engraved and painted. *Opposite* are examples of damascening, a technique of inlaying gold and silver wire on copper, brass and base metals, which reached its peak in the 13th century.

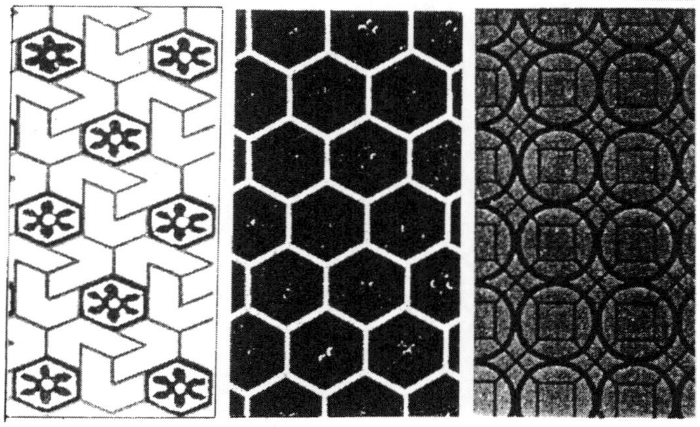

PERSIAN ORNAMENT

A 16thC carpet, featuring the use of the palm leaf; *above left and right* are details from the 'Shah Namah', an illuminated manuscript in the Bibliothèque Nationale, Paris. *Opposite* are ornaments from Persian manuscripts in the British Museum.

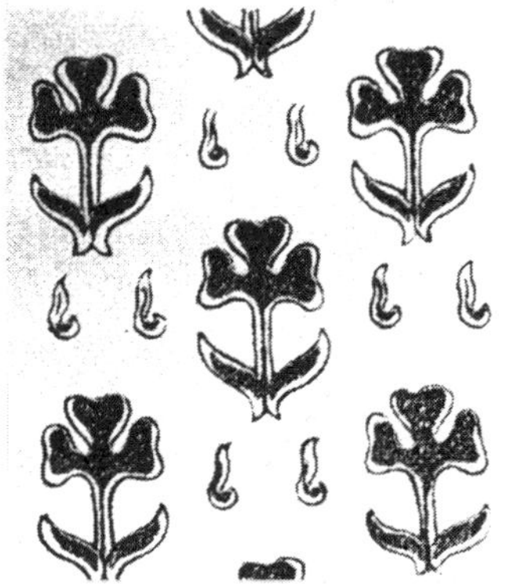

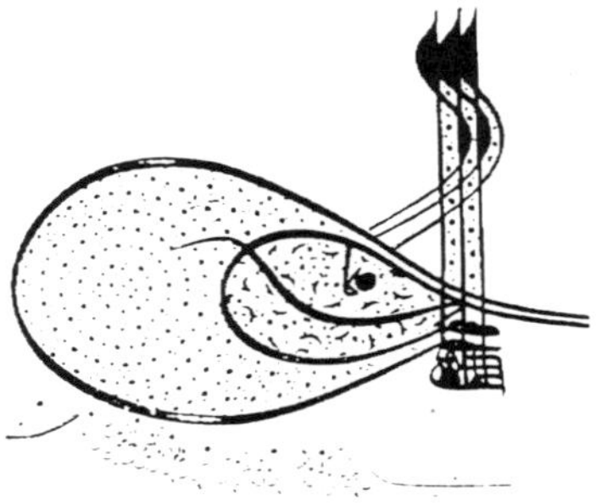

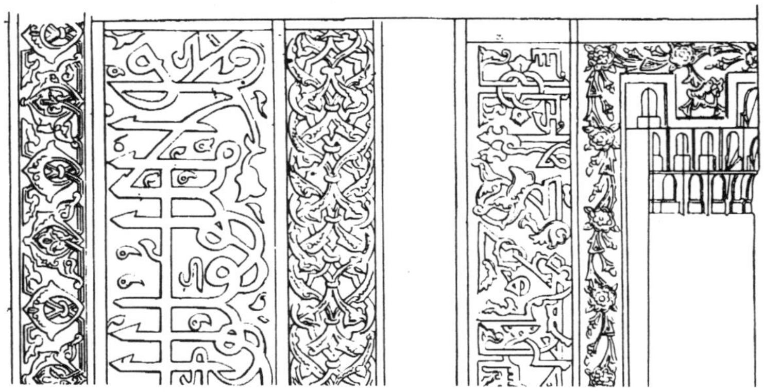

TURKISH ORNAMENT

Calligraphic inscriptions, often quotations from the Koran, are used extensively in Turkish ornament. Sources of examples illustrated include the Yeshil-Jama Mosque at Brusa, and the Medresse of Kari Tai, Konya. The inscriptions represent *top* Suleiman the Magnificent, and *right* the lion of God, symbolizing strength. *Opposite* Persian tiled murals in the dome chamber of the Medresse of Kari Tai *left* and the Medresse Sirtscheh, Konia, *right.*

OTTOMAN TURKISH ORNAMENT

Enamelled glazed tiles, painted enamelled earthenware and marquetry from sites in Istanbul, Brusa and Cairo. The Ottoman empire was founded by Osman I c1300 and lasted until 1919.

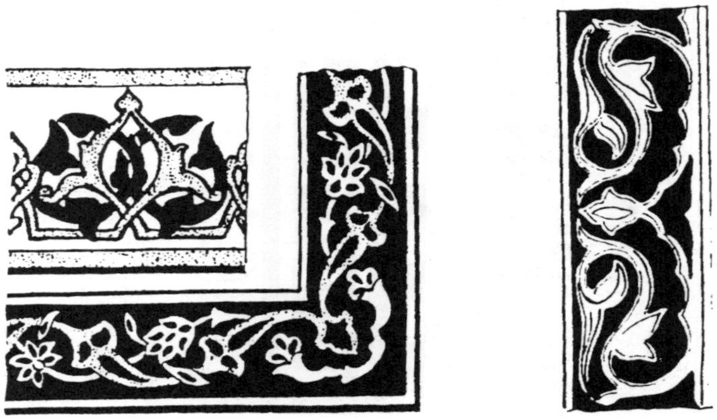

ARMENIAN ORNAMENT

Decorative motifs from Armenian illuminated manuscripts from the 12th to 17th centuries. The motifs display a mixture of Indo-Persian influences, as in the use of floret motifs, with Slavo-Russian characteristics, apparent in the use of interlace.

GEORGIAN ORNAMENT

Details from a selection of Georgian illuminated manuscripts dating from the 12th to 18th centuries. Sources include a 12thC prayer book in the Royal Library, Berlin, and a 17thC book of ritual in the Bibliothèque Nationale, Paris.

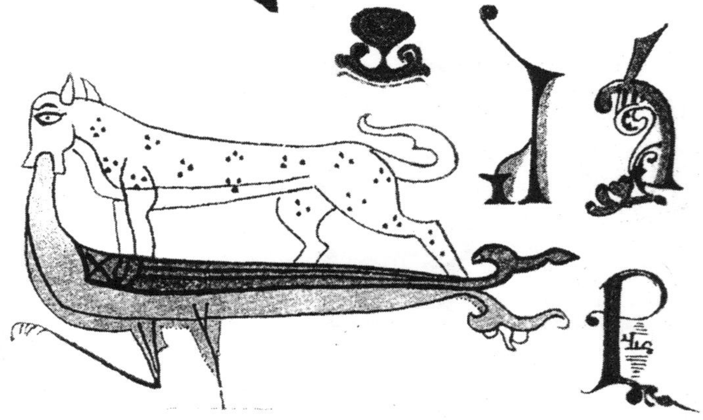

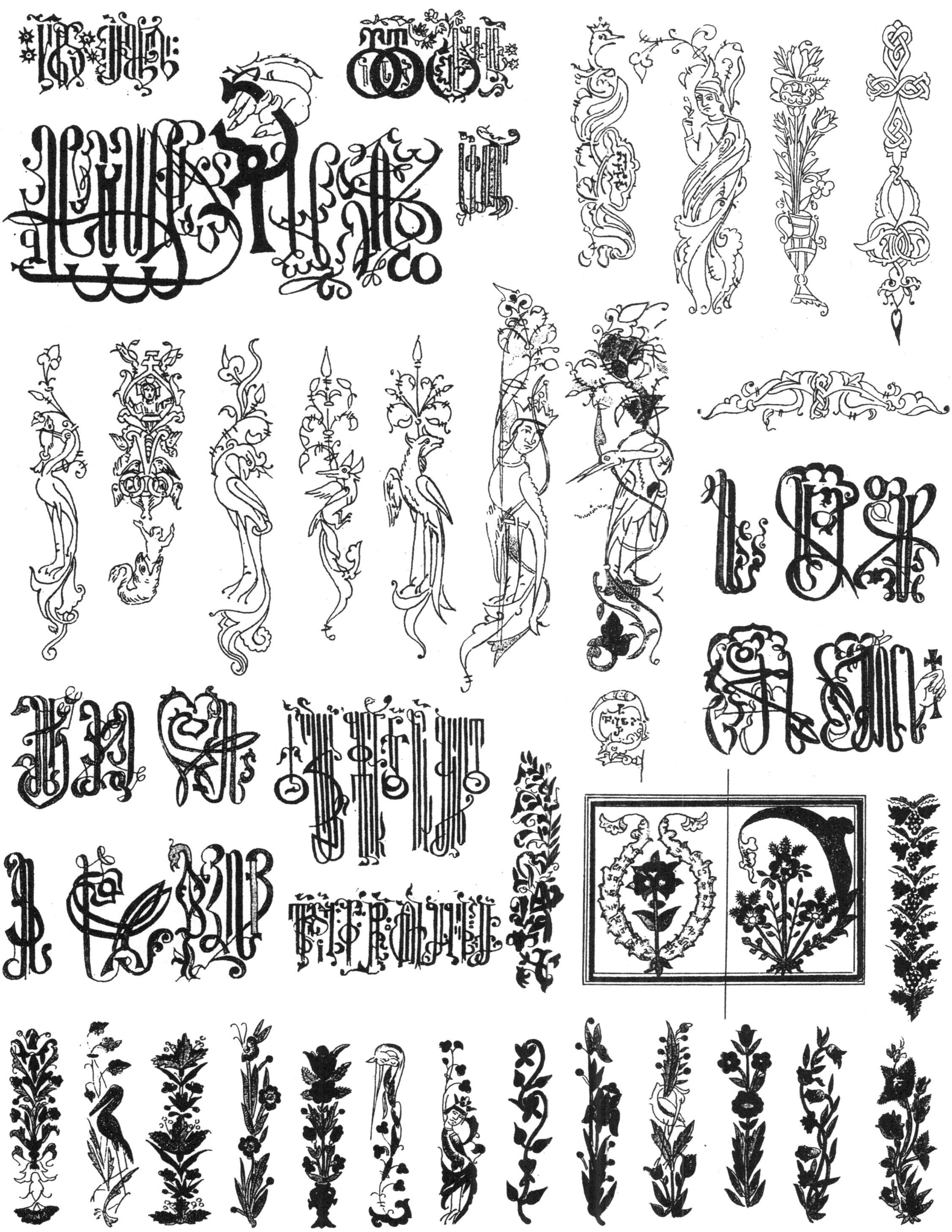

INDIAN ORNAMENT

Above left detail from the temple at Vijayananagar, Dravidian style, 1434; *above centre* detail of a minaret in Ahmedabad, 1430–1450; *top and right* are details of the tomb of Jahangir, Shadara, Lahore. Sources for Indian sculpture and bas-reliefs *opposite* include the temple and great tower of Bhuvanes'war, and the temple of Rajerani.

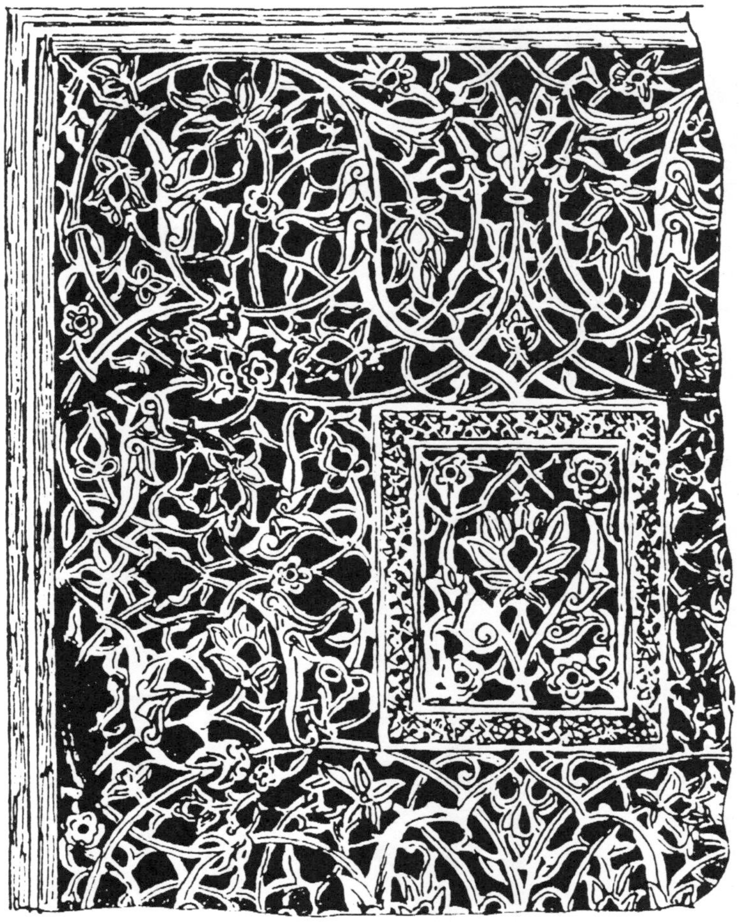

INDIAN MURAL PAINTINGS AND ARCHITECTURAL DECORATION

Details *above left* from the Hindu cave paintings at Ajanta; *above right* pierced panelling in sandstone from Futtipore-Sikri; *right* is a window from a house in Amritsar. *Opposite, l–r* are piers from the mosque Ranee Sipre in Ahmedabad; a column from the palace of the Shah Jahan in Agra; and an arch from the Palace of Amber.

INDIAN ARCHITECTURAL DECORATION

This page shows details of a pierced screen, Bombay Court. *Opposite* is a detail of a carved wooden door from Lahore City.

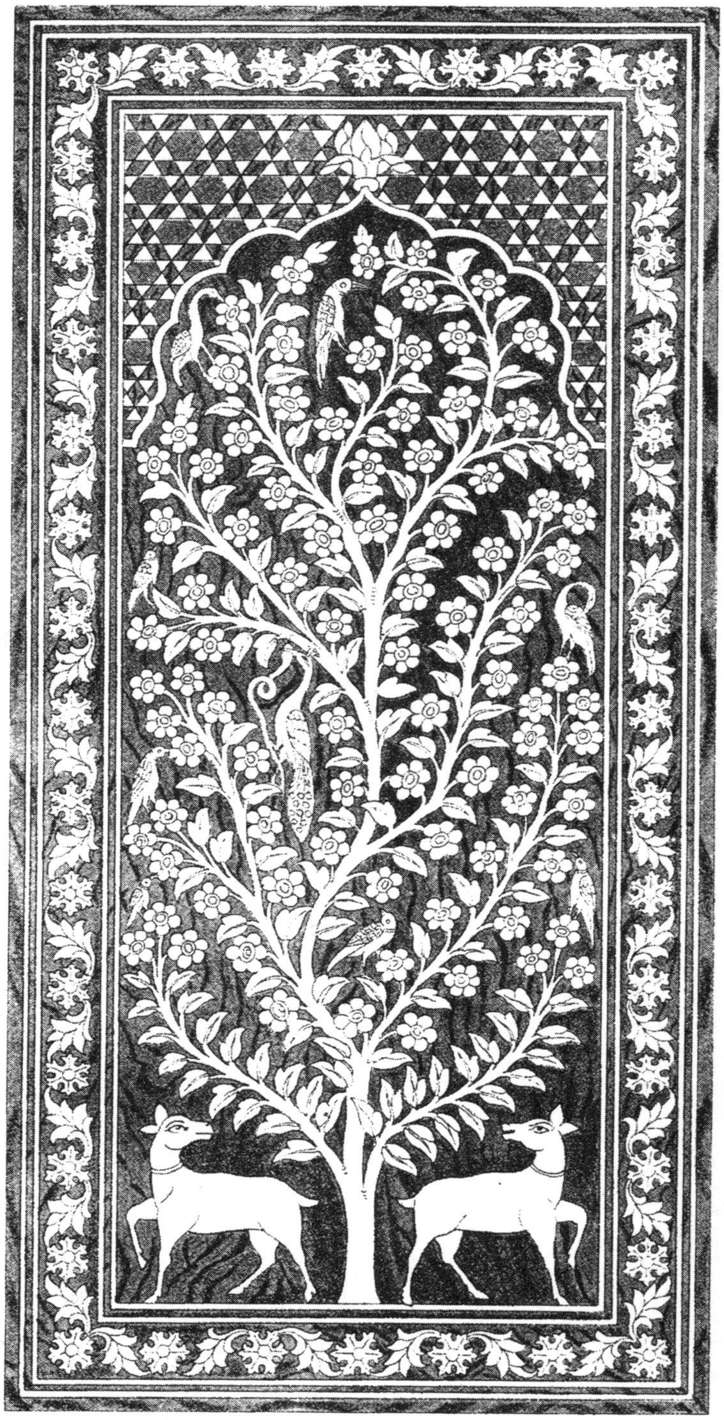

INDIAN ARCHITECTURAL DECORATION

Panels of ivory and wood mosaic from the Sikh Golden Temple, Amritsar. This decorative technique is known as intarsia, and was popular throughout the Indian sub-continent, used both for architectural cladding and panelling, shown here, and for smaller decorative items, such as boxes.

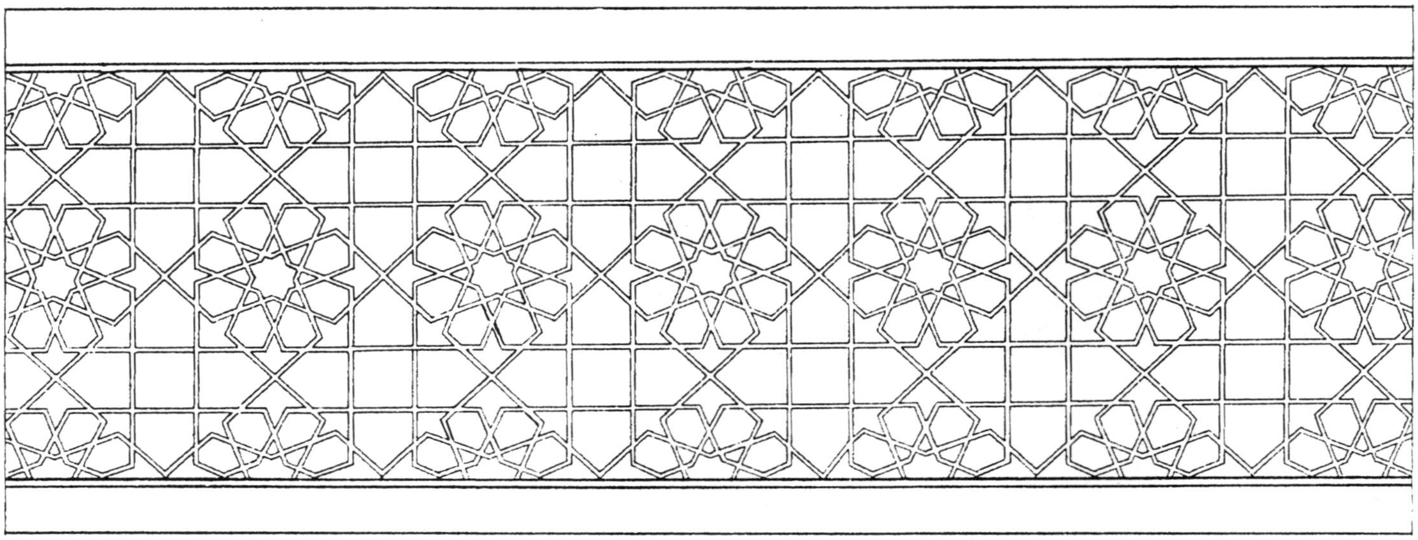

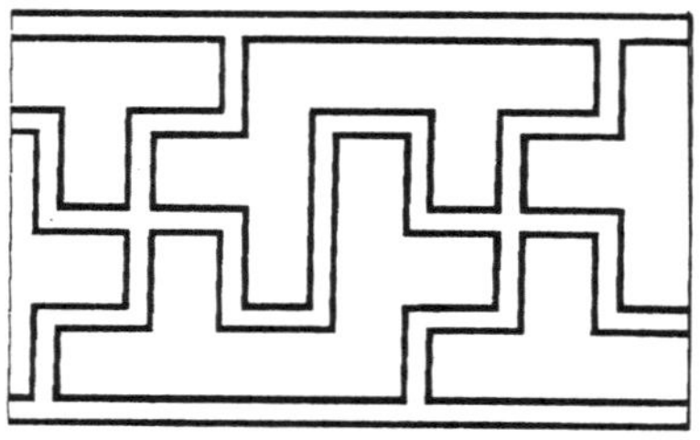

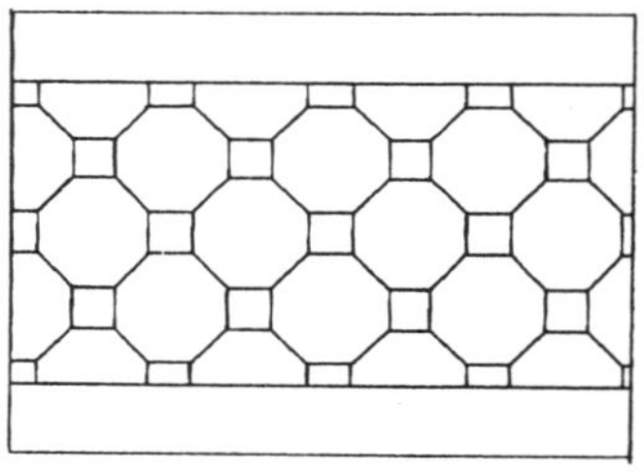

INDIAN ARCHITECTURAL DECORATION

Details of the decoration of the tomb of Jahangir at Shadara, Lahore: designs for marble and stone cladding used on the walls of the tomb, and *opposite* details of frescoes and mosaics.

INDIAN DECORATION

Above and opposite top are painted ceiling decorations from the tomb of Itmad-ud-Daulah, Agra. The other illustrations are designs for enamels from Jaipur, intended for the backs of daggers or hunting knives.

INDIAN DECORATION: JAIPUR ENAMELS

Sword scabbards and *above centre* a dagger sheath. *Opposite* are bracelets and sword scabbard mounts.

INDIAN ORNAMENT

Details from a Hindu carved basalt statue of Surga dating from between the 5th and 9th centuries (Royal Asiatic Society). *Opposite* are examples of Indian metalwork and jewellery, including enamelled copper, cloisonné enamel, engraving in niello, and chasing on steel. The enamelled gold pendant *top centre* is from Rajputana.

INDIAN EMBROIDERY

This page shows embroidered borders from Reshmi-Bharat-Kam. *Opposite* is a detail of an embroidered sari in Phulcari (flower work), from Amritsar.

TIBETAN PAINTING AND BRONZES AND NEPALESE JEWELLERY

A painting *top* and gilt bronzes *above* of the incarnate Gods of Tibet; *right* is a steel and tinder case with silver and coral mountings. *Opposite* are copper and silver prayer-wheels, gold and silver shirt-clasps, a charm box and a ring, a silver charm box *bottom left,* and a libation bowl, made of a skull, with base and cover of gilded bronze.

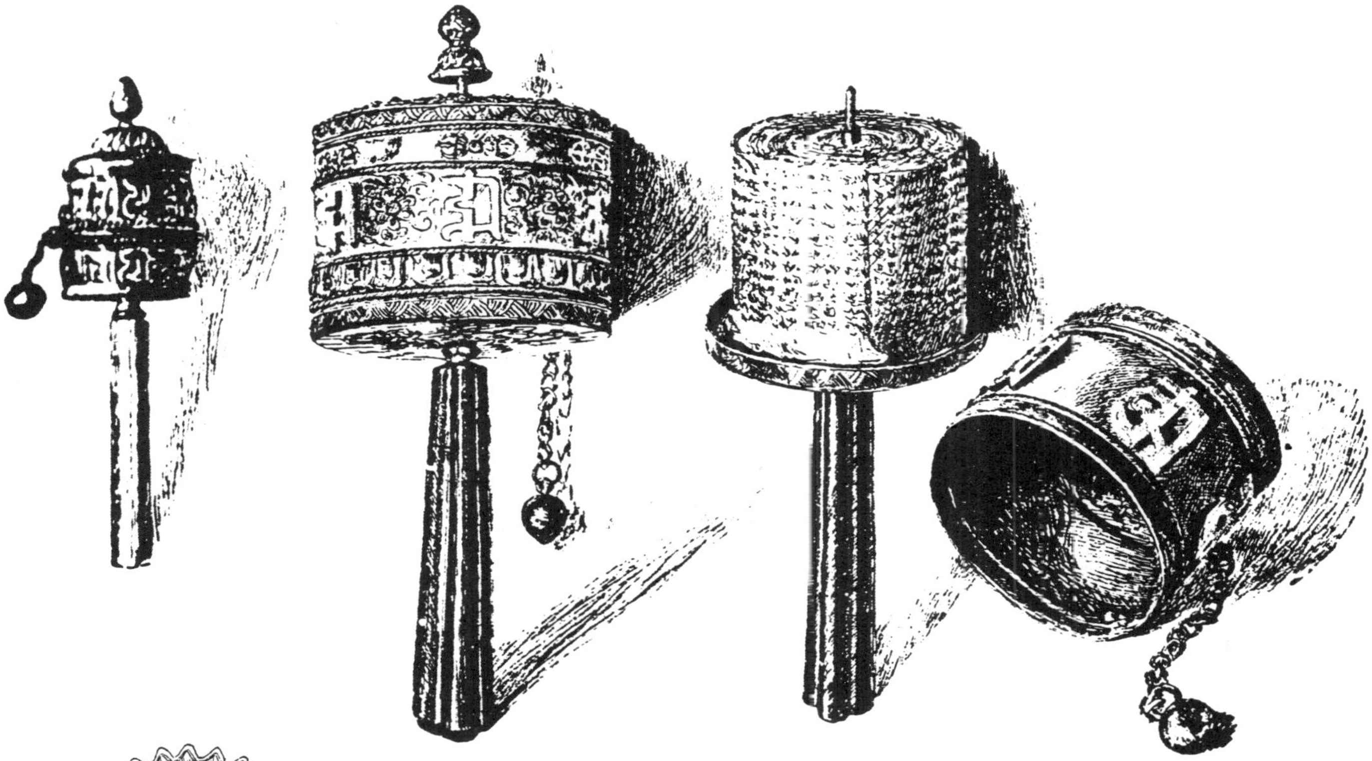

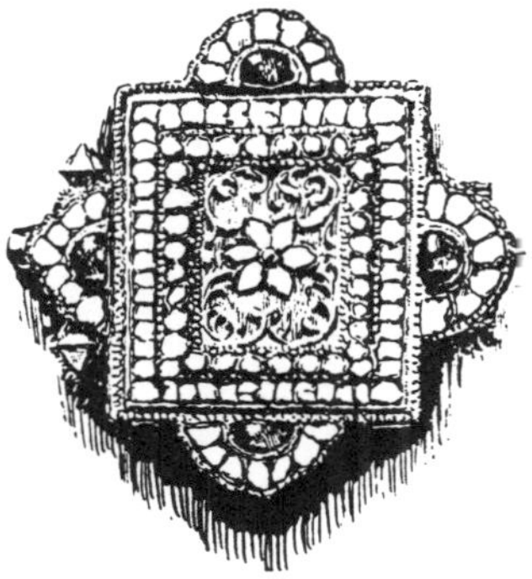

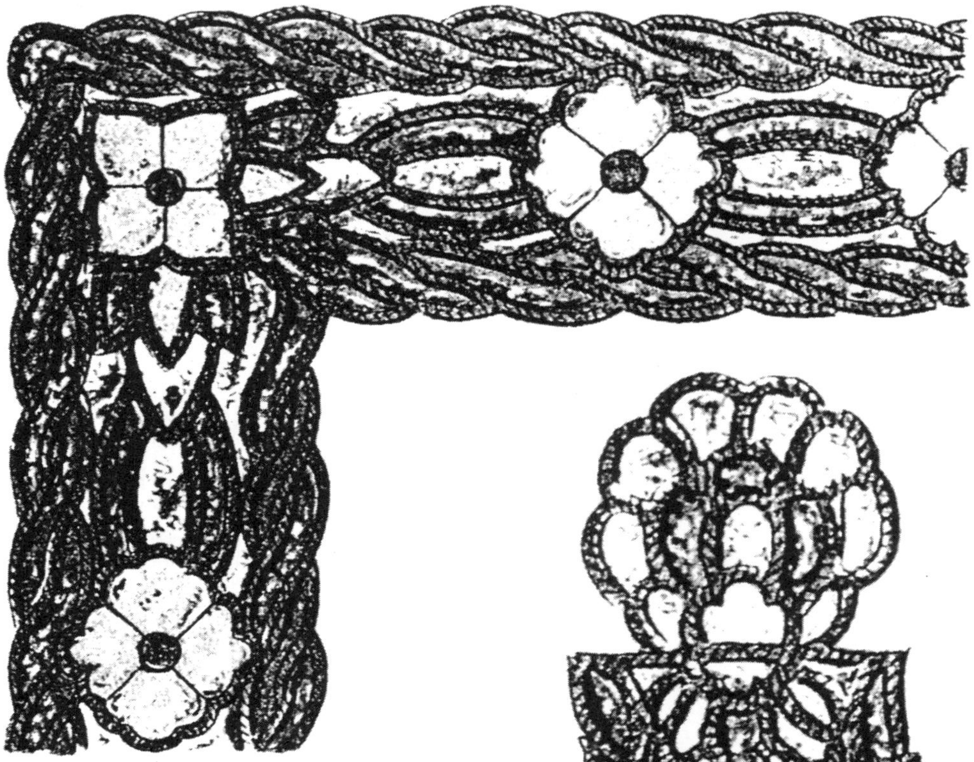

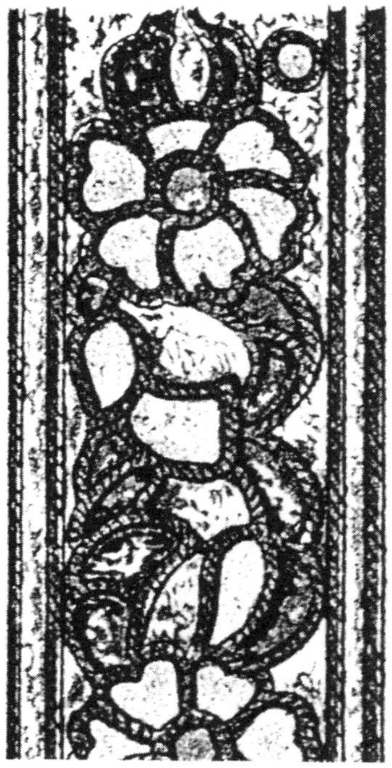

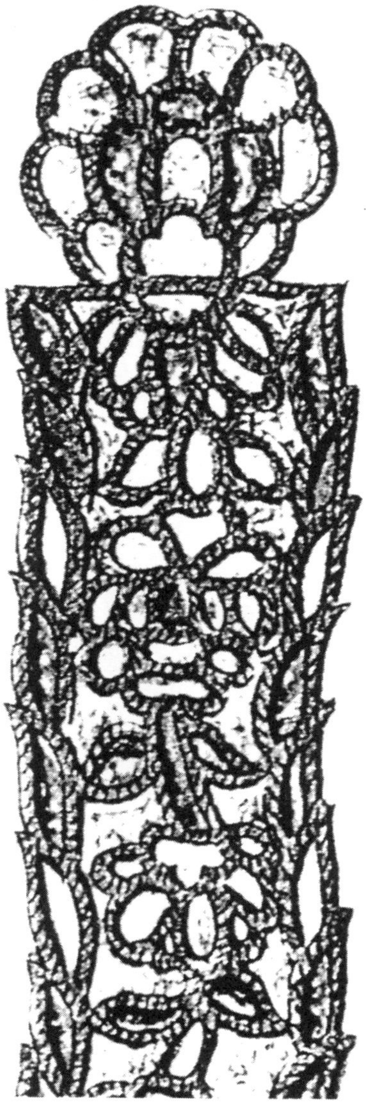

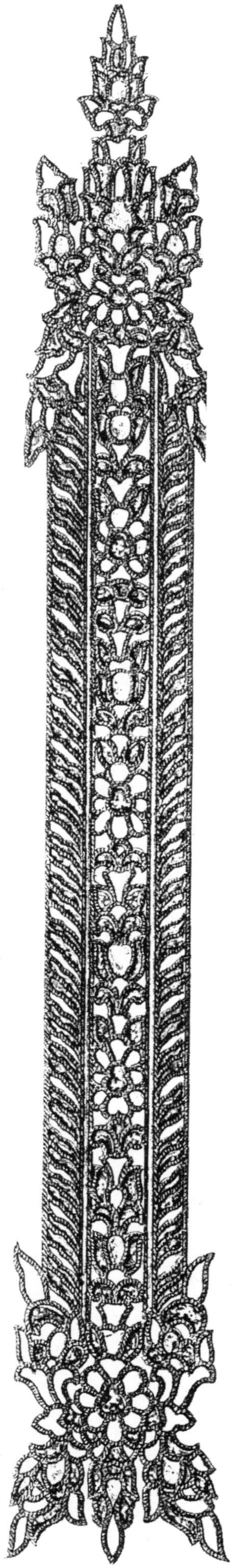

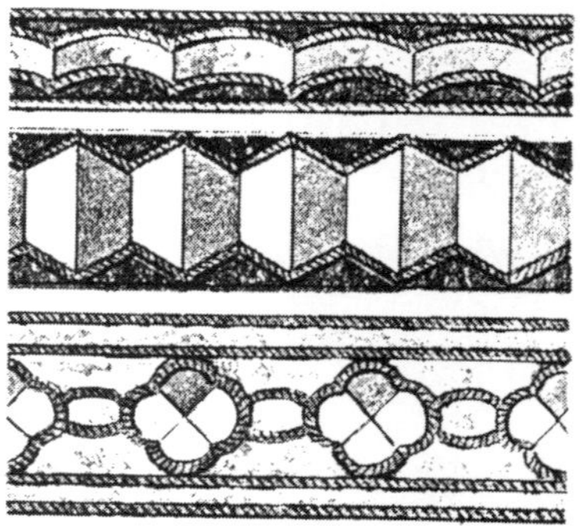

BURMESE ORNAMENT

Details of decoration from Burmese shrines, and a Burmese standard, exhibited at the Crystal Palace, London, in 1855. *Opposite* are details of Burmese wood carvings, from the collections first published by Owen Jones in 1856.

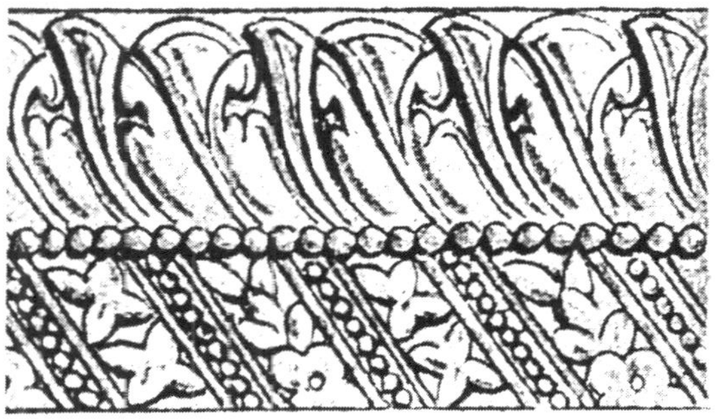

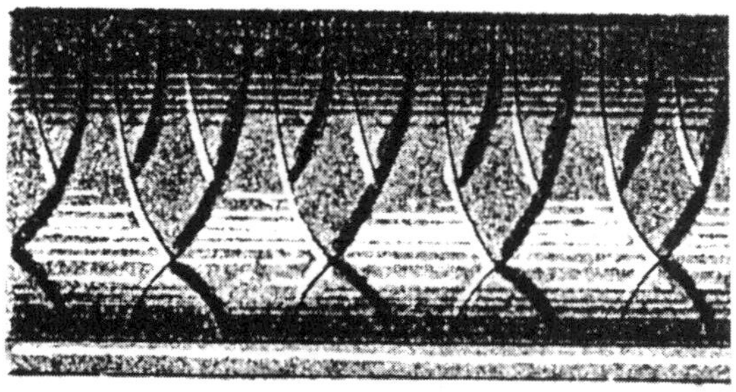

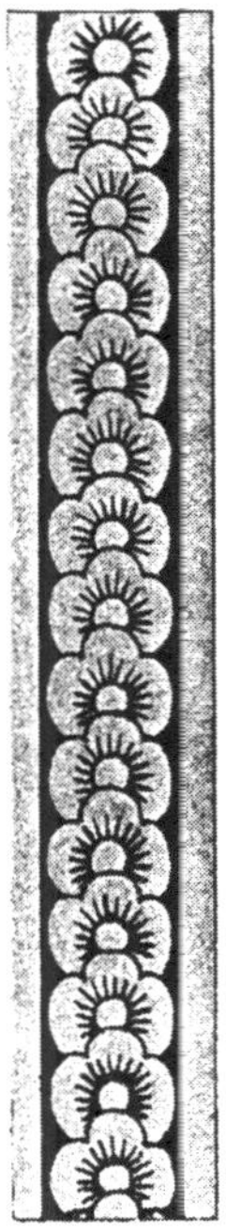

CAMBODIAN ORNAMENT

Details of carved decoration from the 10thC Temple of Angkor Wat. *Opposite left* is a doorway of the 11thC Temple of Loley, and *right* a square pier and entablature with frieze representing the Apsaras (celestial dancing girls) from the Temple of Angkor Wat.

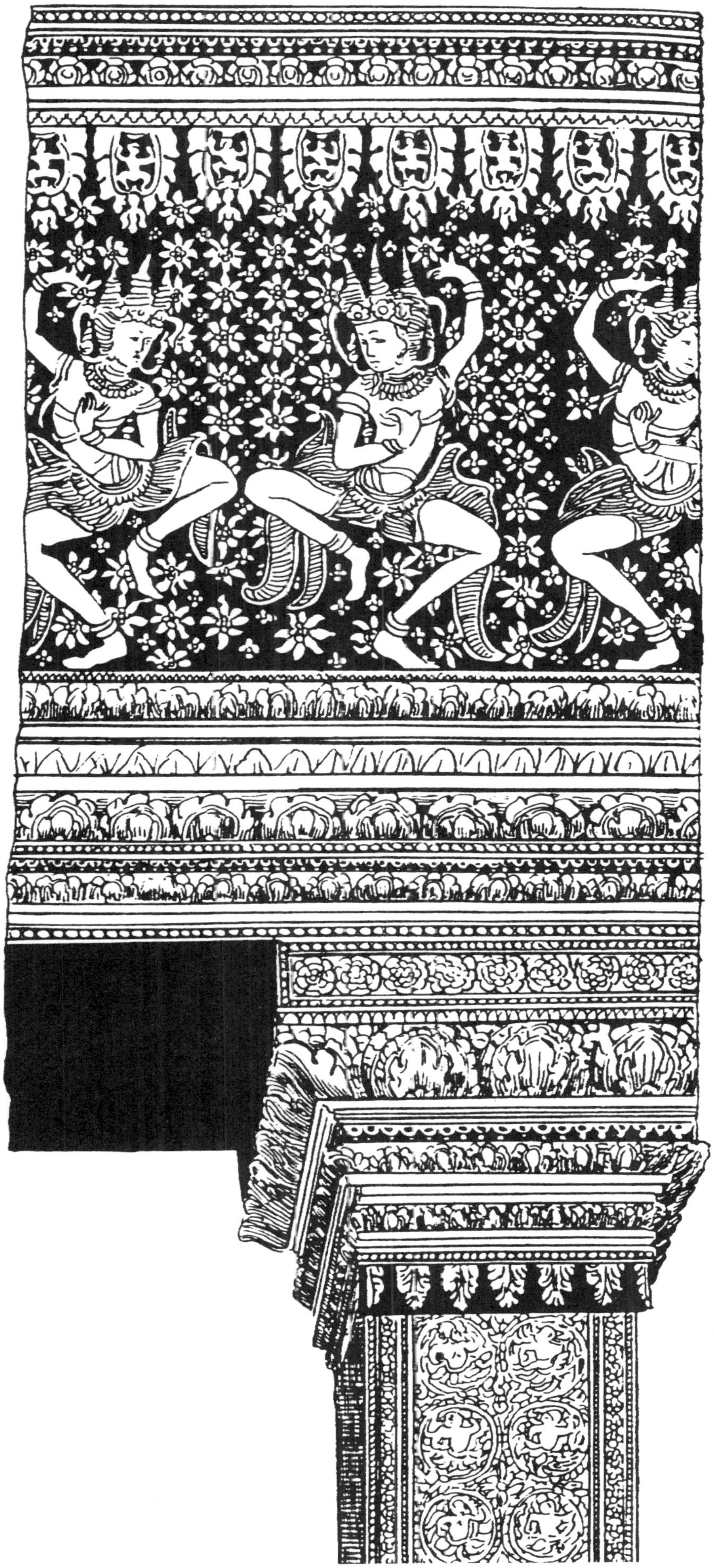

CHINESE ORNAMENT

This page shows the decorative pattern from a painted china vase, using the continuous stem principle of decoration. *Opposite* is the decoration of a painted china bottle, combining continuous stem decoration with detached emblems, scattered over the surface.

CHINESE ORNAMENT

Detail of the decoration of a Chinese blue and white china bottle. *Opposite* are details of decoration from Chinese blue and white ceramics. The central roundel and the borders *top* display Persian influence.

CHINESE ORNAMENT

This page shows part of the decoration of a painted china bottle, cast in a mould. The composition is on the continuous-stem principle, and the ornament is in slight relief. *Opposite* are details of decoration from painted china, a dish in the form of a star and a panel, both displaying Indian influence.

CHINESE ORNAMENT

The decoration of a china bottle, showing continuous stem pattern. Designs of this type became sources for William Morris. *Opposite* is part of a pendant ornament round the top of a blue and white cistern, also using the continuous stem principle. The flowers are arranged geometrically; their shaded graphic representation is Indian in character.

CHINESE ORNAMENT

A series of borders taken from examples of blue and white ceramics demonstrates how certain forms of pattern, such as the meander, the foliate scroll and the lotus flower, all common in other cultures, are all used internationally.

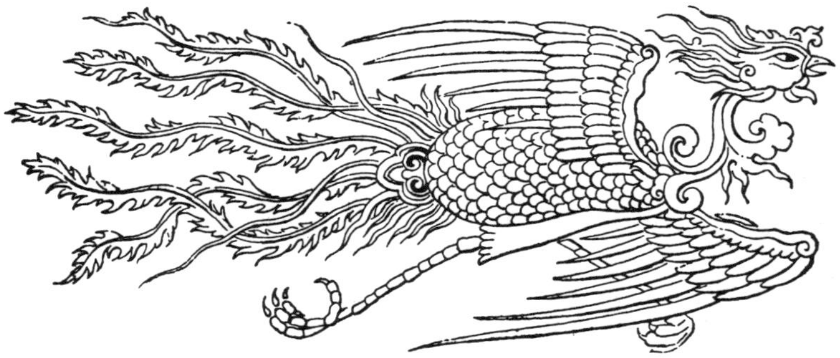

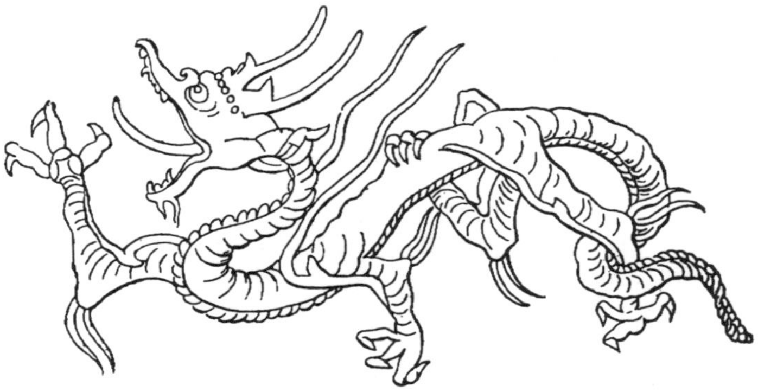

CHINESE ORNAMENT

Top is a fragment of embroidery. In the original, white lines are used to accentuate the design, against the yellow ochre background. *Above and right* are three mythological Chinese creatures: the fong-hoang, the dragon and Fo's dog. *Opposite* are mid 19thC designs in the Chinese manner by John Leighton.

CHINESE ORNAMENT

The peony *top left* symbolizes wealth; the chrysanthemum *top right* endurance; *above and right* are birds and flowers symbolizing happiness. The cock *opposite top left* represents courage and reliability; the tiger *top right* fierceness and courage; the dragon *centre* was the personal symbol of Chinese emperors, representing a link with heaven.

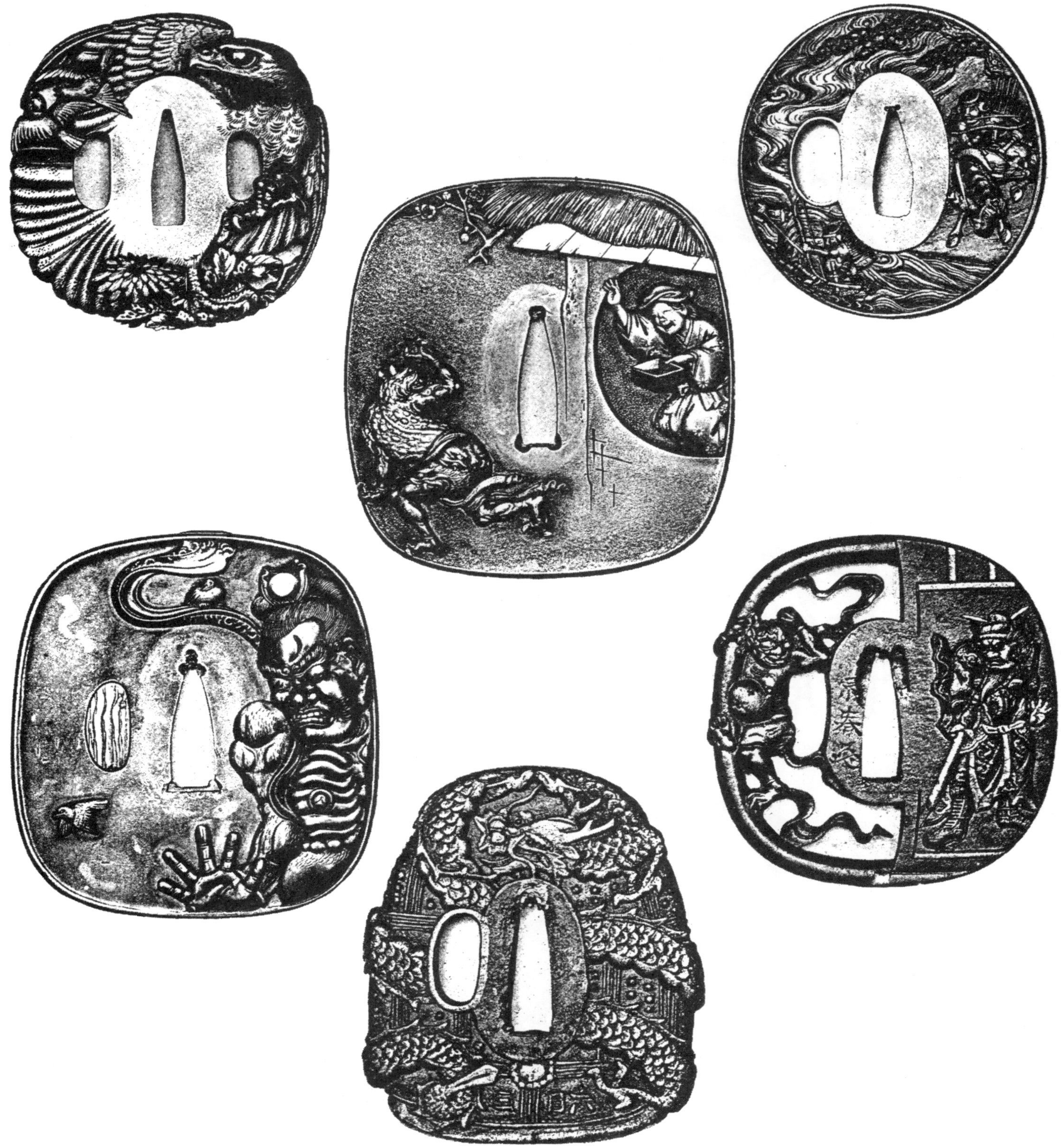

JAPANESE SWORD GUARDS AND ENAMELS

This page shows 16th – 18thC sword guards, in pierced and chased iron, some also inlaid with gold, silver and copper. *Opposite* are examples of cloisonné enamel, taken from a copper dish: a section of the complete dish top, and individual details.

JAPANESE FLORA AND FAUNA

Top left is a decorated initial showing the actor Tomejuro Nakamura in the role of Kaishi, painted by Tori-i-Kiyo-nobu (1750). The other images are floral designs featuring the peony and plum. *Opposite* are a crayfish *top*, a bat *right*, three images of cranes, and *bottom right* a jay.

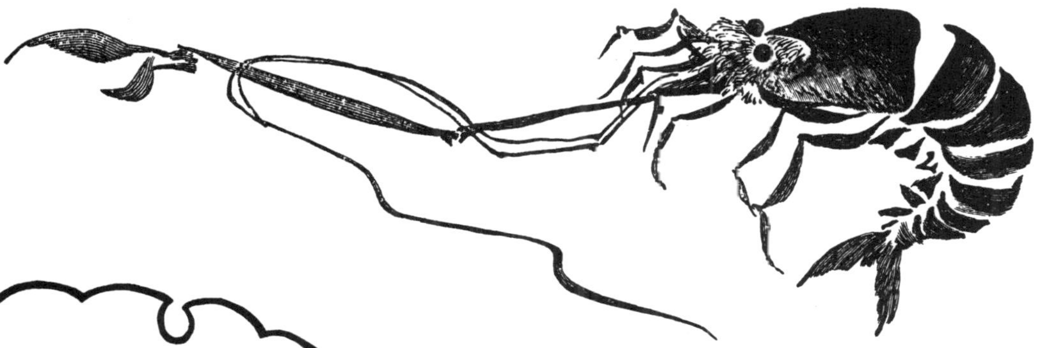

JAPANESE FISH

Next to birds, fish are one of the most popular subjects for Japanese artists. These images represent both naturalistic and stylized treatments of carp.

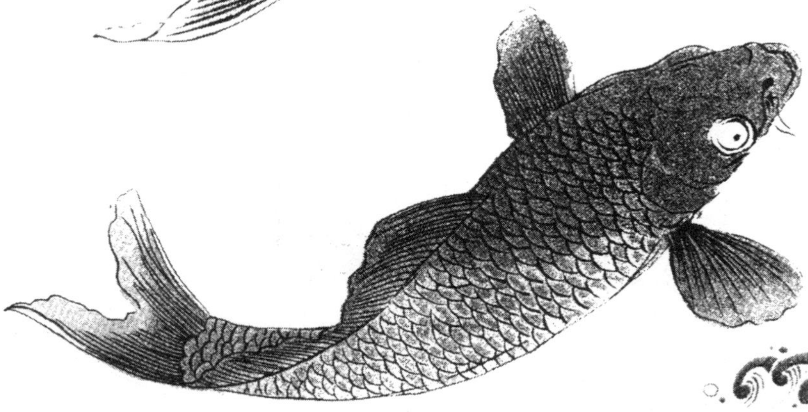

JAPANESE ORNAMENT

A selection of designs in the Japanese manner, compiled by John Leighton. During the 1870s and 1880s, through designers such as Dresser, Godwin and Tiffany, Japanese design had a strong influence on Western taste.

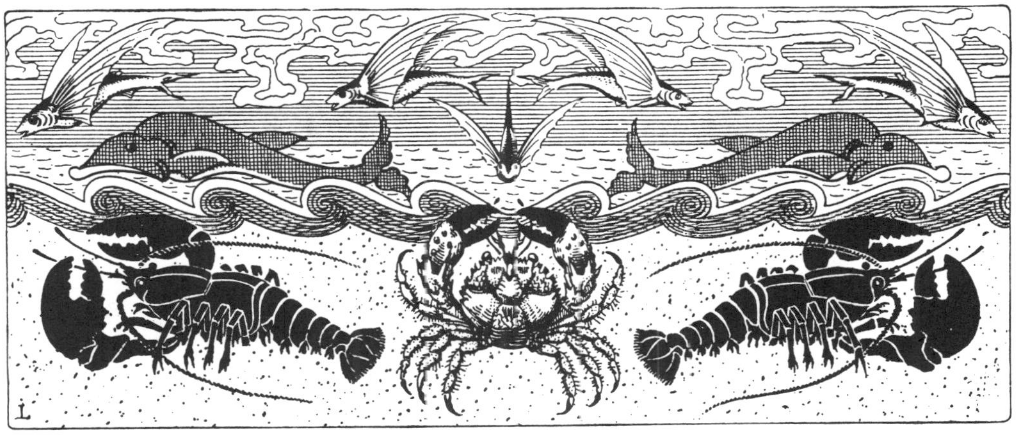

JAPANESE PLANTS

A selection of Japanese plants, showing both conventional and naturalistic treatments, including cherries, chrysanthemums, plums and bamboo. Japanese artists learnt to paint motifs like these by copying existing models rather than working directly from nature.

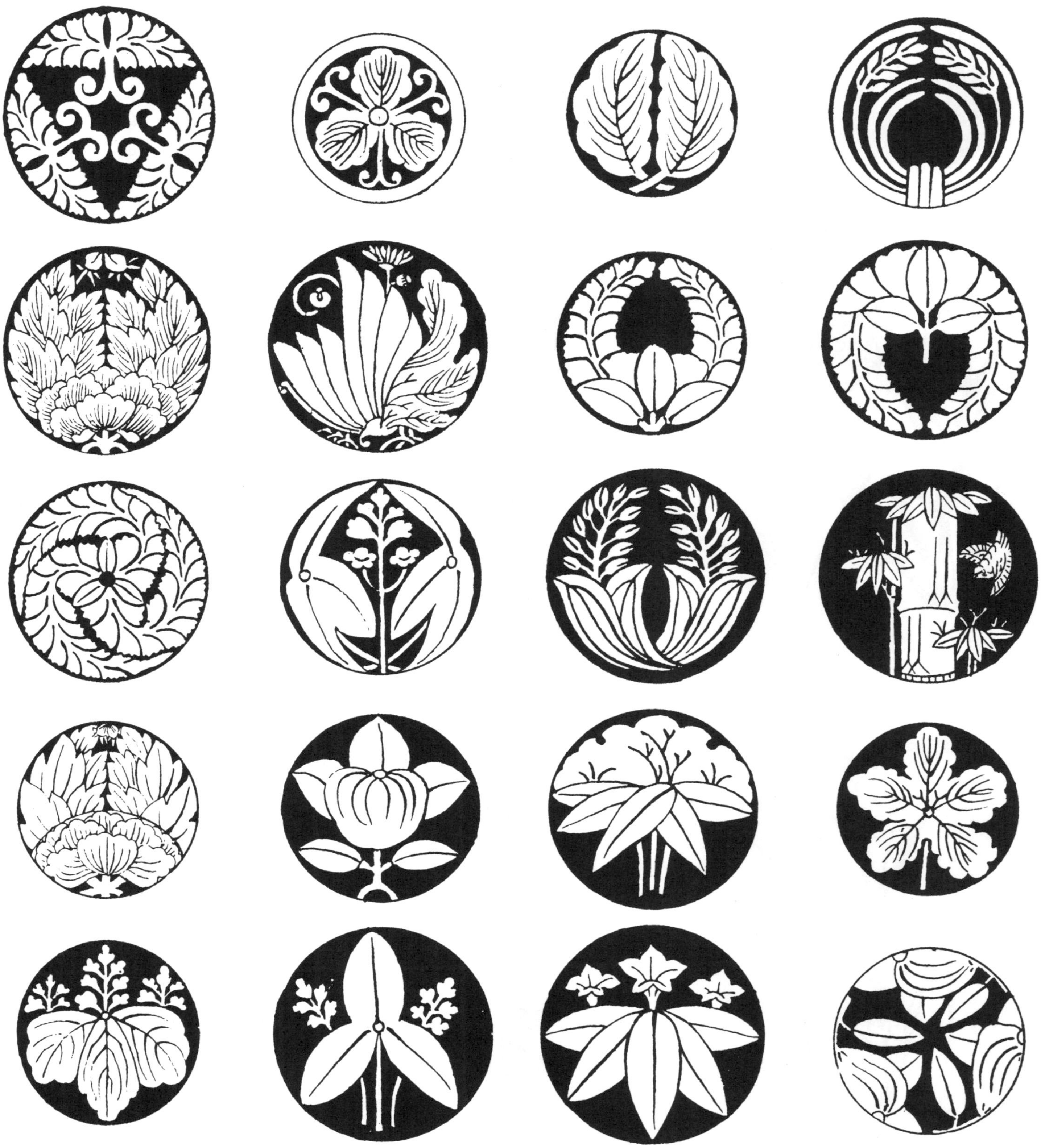

JAPANESE ORNAMENT

On *this page* and *overleaf* a selection of designs for Japanese noblemen's badges, showing stylized representations of a variety of flowers, insects, birds and a bat, demonstrates the Japanese genius for pattern within confined spaces.

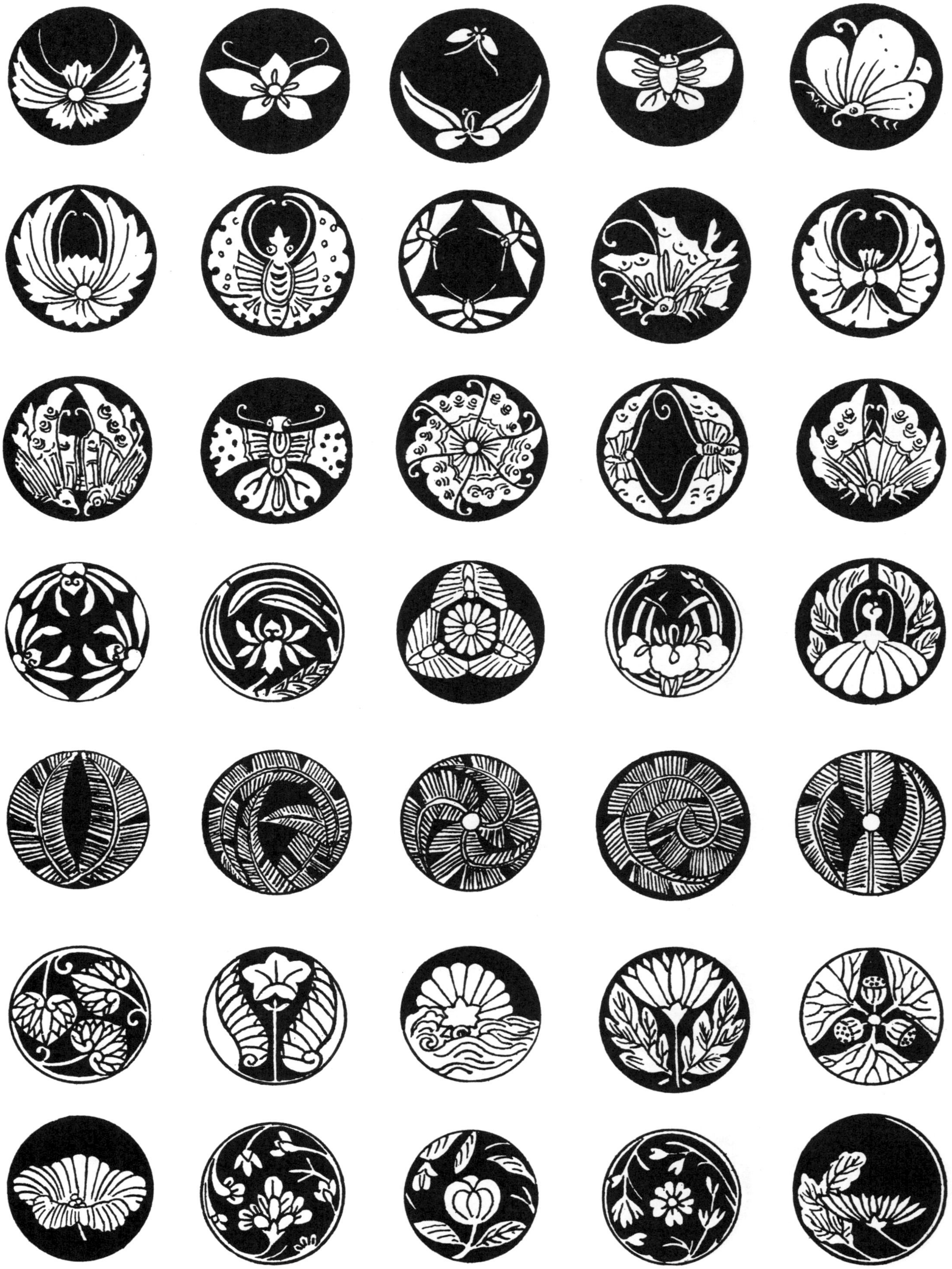

JAPANESE SURFACE PATTERN

A selection of Japanese designs for flat pattern, suitable for use for both textiles and wallpaper. *Opposite bottom centre* is a design apparently from a ceremonial bridal gown: in a traditional Japanese marriage ceremony, the role of the bridesmaids is to flutter back and forth between the two parties, like the butterflies graphically depicted in this design.

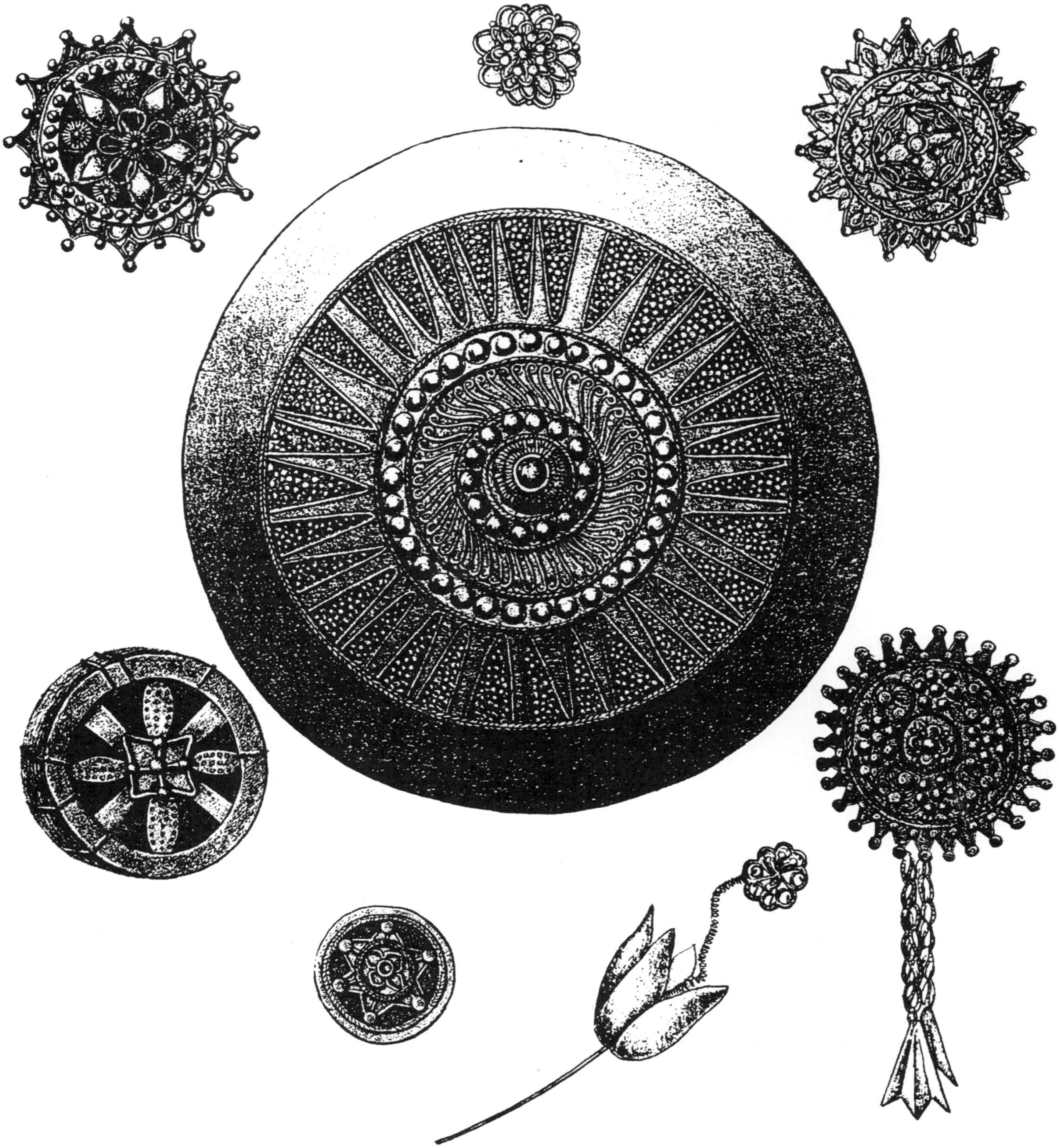

SUMATRAN METALWORK

A selection of metalwork collected by a Dutch expedition to Sumatra and Indonesia in the 1870s. The fine gold and silver jewellery uses such techniques as granulation and filigree work.

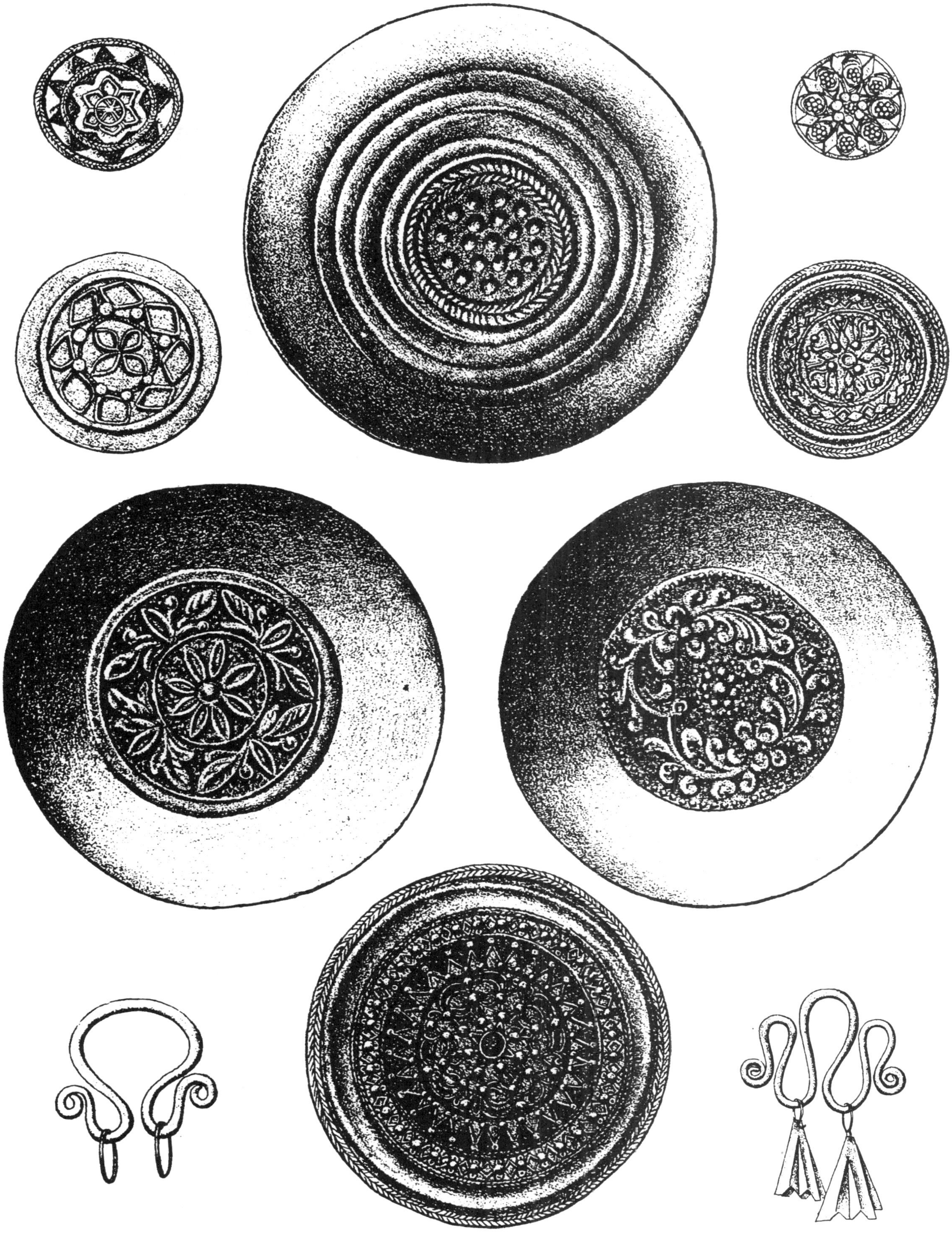

SUMATRAN CRAFTS

Above a selection of Sumatran jewellery and *opposite* Sumatran beakers and lidded boxes, spindles and pipes. The lidded boxes, in which betel nuts are stored, are carved from gourds.

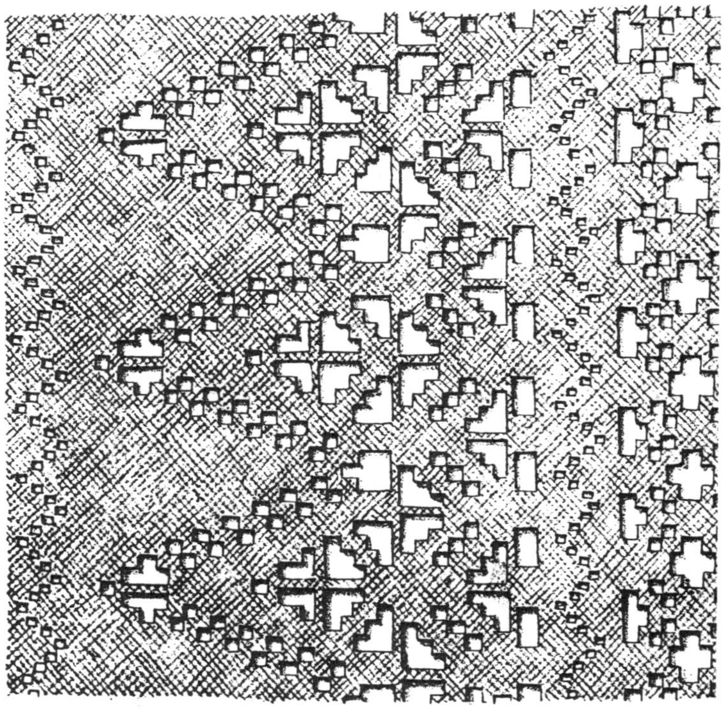

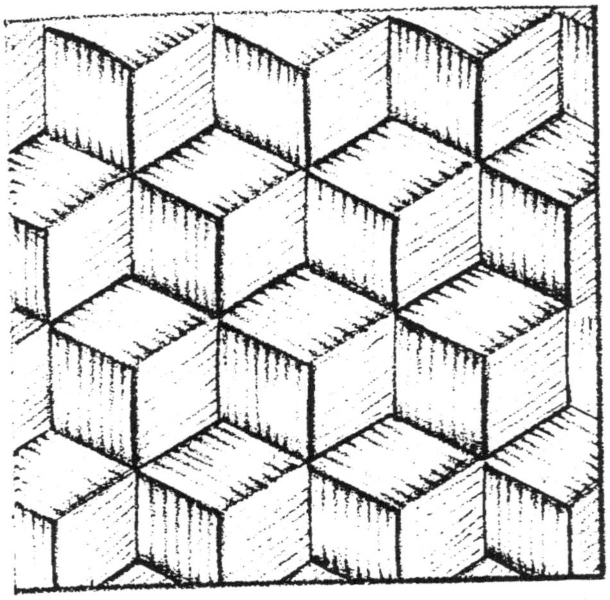

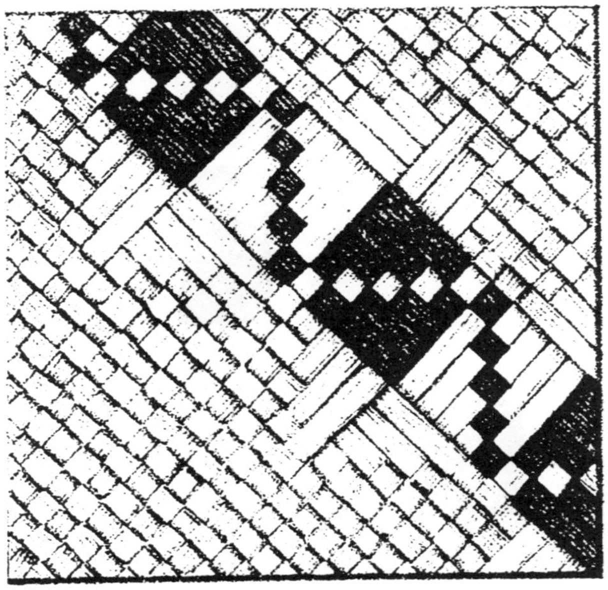

SUMATRAN CRAFTS

Examples of Sumatran basketwork, showing both woven work and a detail *above* of a finely woven fine mat, with characteristic geometric pierced designs. Mats of this type were used as wall hangings in Sumatran homes.

AFRICA

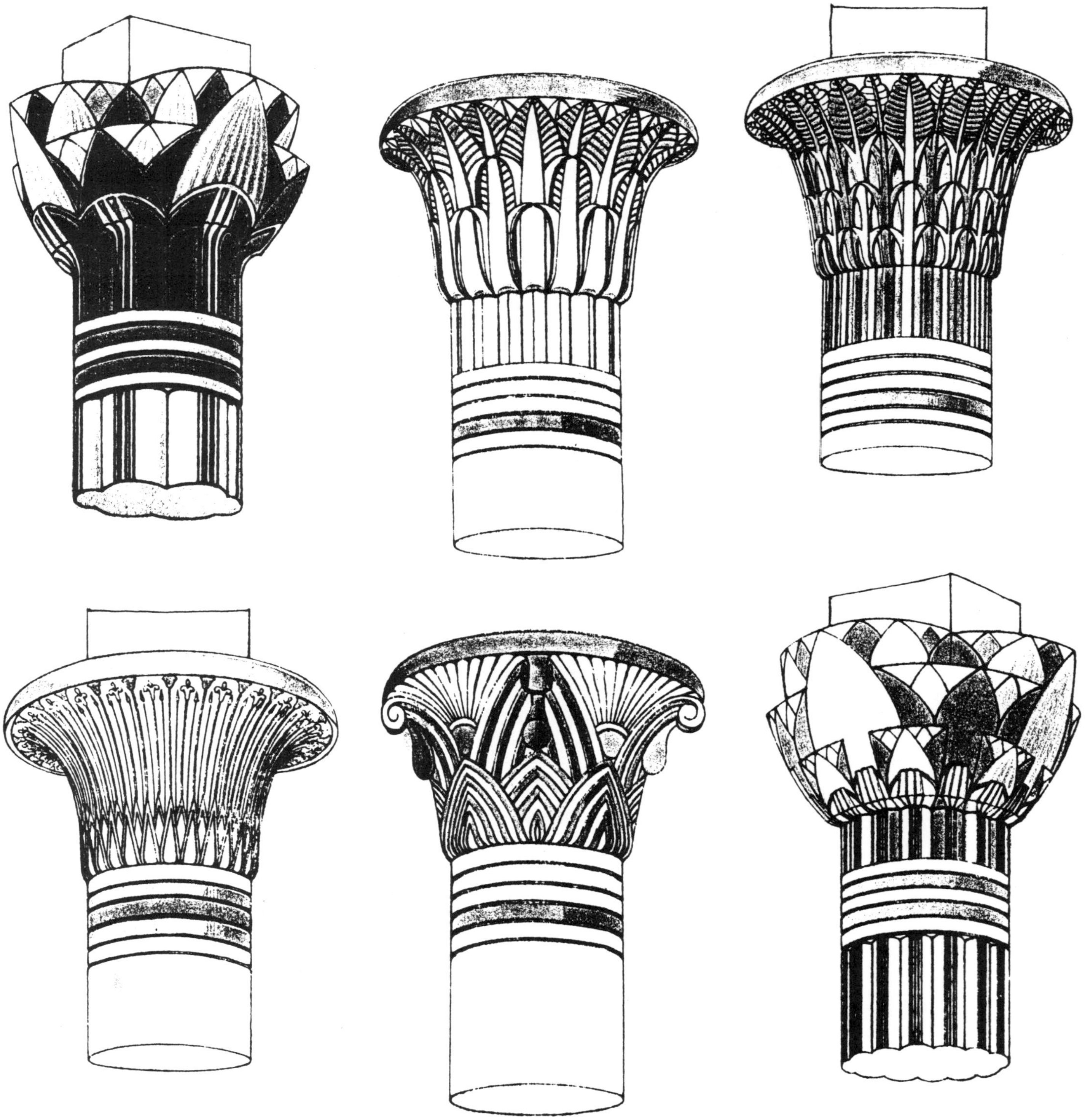

EGYPTIAN CAPITALS

These demonstrate the strictly systematic arrangements of native plants in Egyptian ornament, using the leaves and flowers of the lotus, lily, papyrus, date-palm and reeds. Temples represented the world, ceilings symbolized the sky, columns and capitals represented the stalks and flowers of plants. Sources show temples at Thebes, including the temple of Luxor, c1250 BC, *top left and opposite centre;* temples on the island of Philae *above left and right* and *opposite top left and top centre;* the portico of Edfu, 145 BC, *top right;* and the temple of Koom-Ombos *opposite bottom right.*

EGYPTIAN ORNAMENT

This page shows feathers, dried leaves and lotus leaves used for fans and head-dresses; a gold and enamelled vase in the form of the lotus *centre;* and boats made from papyrus leaves bound together *above. Opposite* are schematic treatments of lotus and papyrus leaves, including *centre* a column combining the two, bound together with matting and ribbons, and *bottom centre* the lotus and papyrus growing in the Nile.

EGYPTIAN JEWELLERY, PAINTING AND RELIEF

Top centre a cloisonné enamel breastplate, dating from the reign of Rameses II, XIX dynasty; *top left and right* details of jewellery from paintings at Thebes; *centre* a scarab with a lapiz lazuli head and wings of glass beads. *Opposite bottom left and right* are front and side views of a caryatid representing Rameses Sesotris, from the rock-cut temple of Phre at Ibsamboul; *bottom centre right* is a profile of seated woman on throne: her klaft (head-dress) is topped by an additional head-dress representing Hathor, the Egyptian Venus.

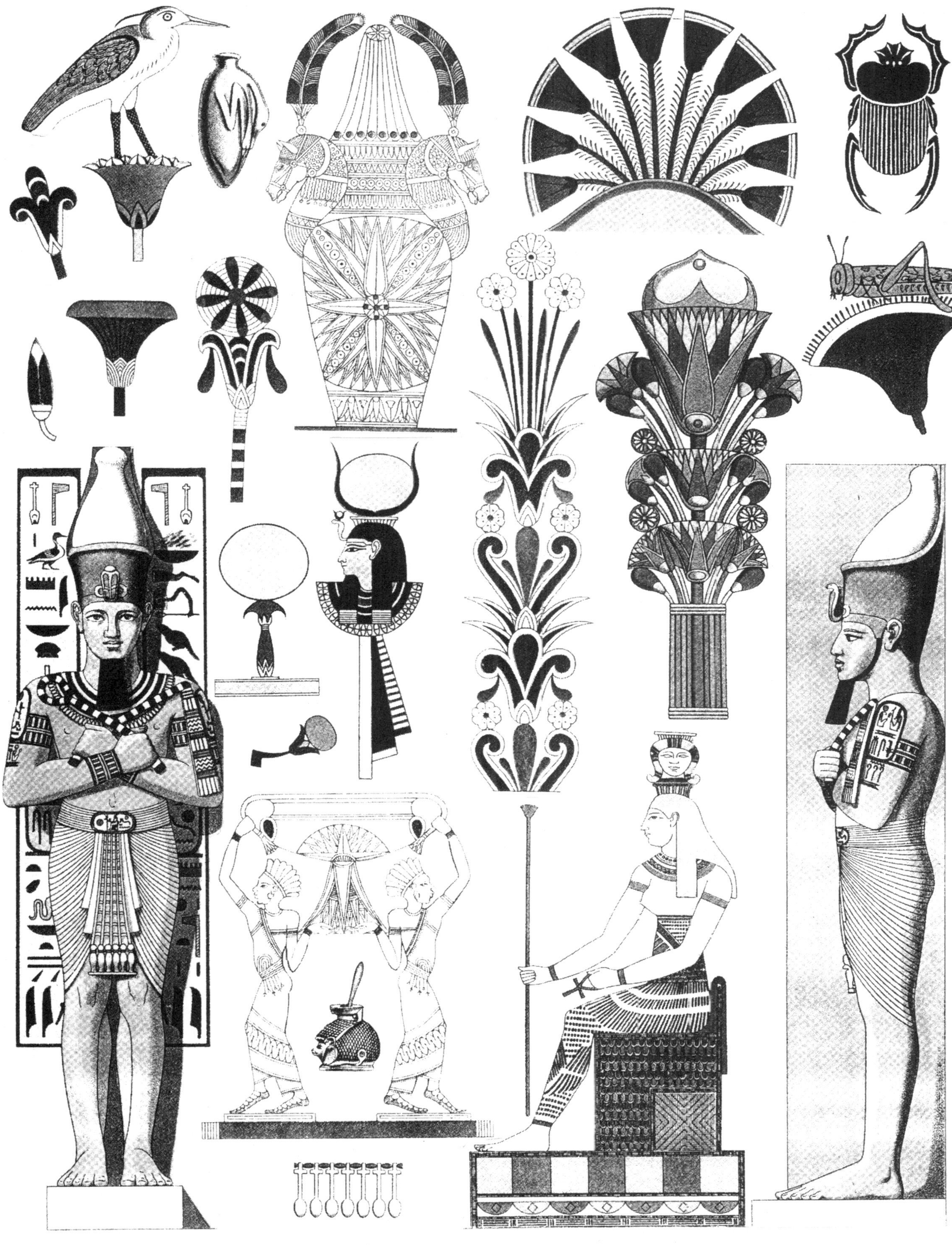

EGYPTIAN SURFACE DESIGN

This page shows a selection of flat repeat patterns. Although these make frequent use of scrolls, they nonetheless have a strong and tightly structured geometric emphasis. The guilloches and meanders *opposite bottom left, lower centre and bottom right* date from the XVI to XX dynasties.

ISLAMIC ORNAMENT

Opposite are wooden window screens from the 14thC mosque of Quawsun. *This page* shows a selection of Machrabiyyah (wooden fretwork grilles).

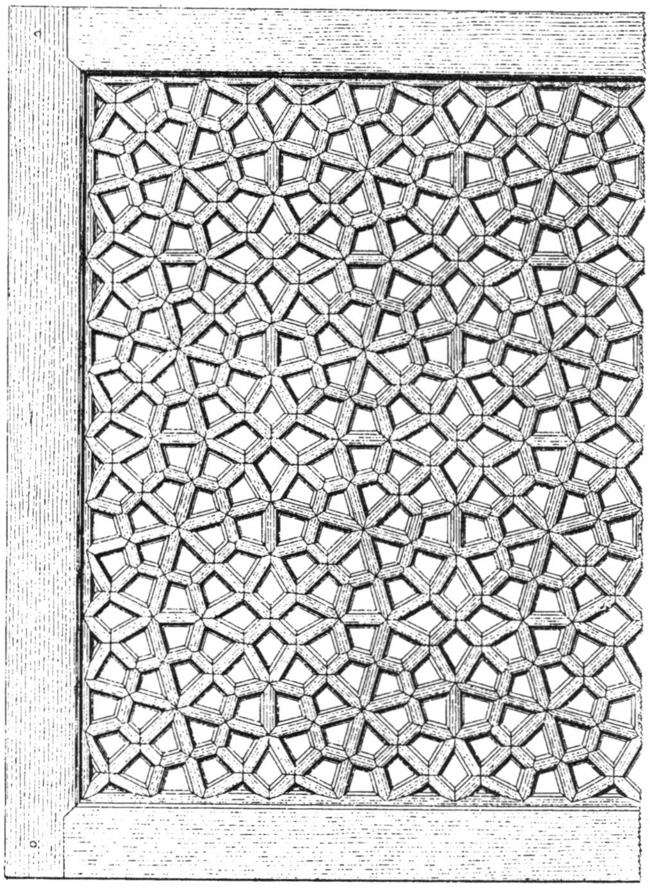

ISLAMIC ARCHITECTURAL ORNAMENT

This page shows details from the mosques of Sultan Kalaoon and En Nasrireeyeh, Cairo. The former was founded in 1284–5. All the ornaments are in carved plaster, which appears to have been cut while still wet. *Opposite* are columns and pillars dating from between the 9th and 15th centuries.

ISLAMIC GEOMETRIC ORNAMENT

Designs like these are used widely throughout Islamic architecture for surface patterns, in marble and ceramics for mosaics and for wall and floor tiles, and also for ivory and wood inlay, known as intarsia. The examples *this page* date from the 15th and 16th centuries. *Opposite* are details of geometric wall mosaics from the mosque of Al-Burdayni, from the end of the 17th century.

ARAB ORNAMENT

Examples of designs for stucco inlay into a bed of white marble, dating from the 16th to 18th centuries, and *opposite* friezes and borders from the ante-rooms of the mosque of Al-Burdayni, dating from the end of the 17th century.

MASKS

Masks and icons form an important element in African tribal religious ceremonies. *Top, l–r* examples from Cameroon, Congo-Kinshasa, Ivory Coast, Gabon; *above* examples from Kalabar, Yoruba, Liberia. *Opposite top, l–r* are examples from Mali, Congo-Kinshasa, Sudan, Upper Volta, and *far right* from Nigeria, Gabon. Other illustrations show examples from Kalabar, Yoruba and Liberia.

SHIELDS

Shields of the Wakerewe people of Lake Victoria: triangular patterns predominate, and typical colours are black and white, and sometimes red. *Opposite* are shields of the Ushashi people, very similar to those of the Masai and painted in bright colours. Each design is specific to a particular village. These examples were collected by Paul Kollmann in the late 19th century, and are now in the collection of the Museum für Völkerkunde, Berlin.

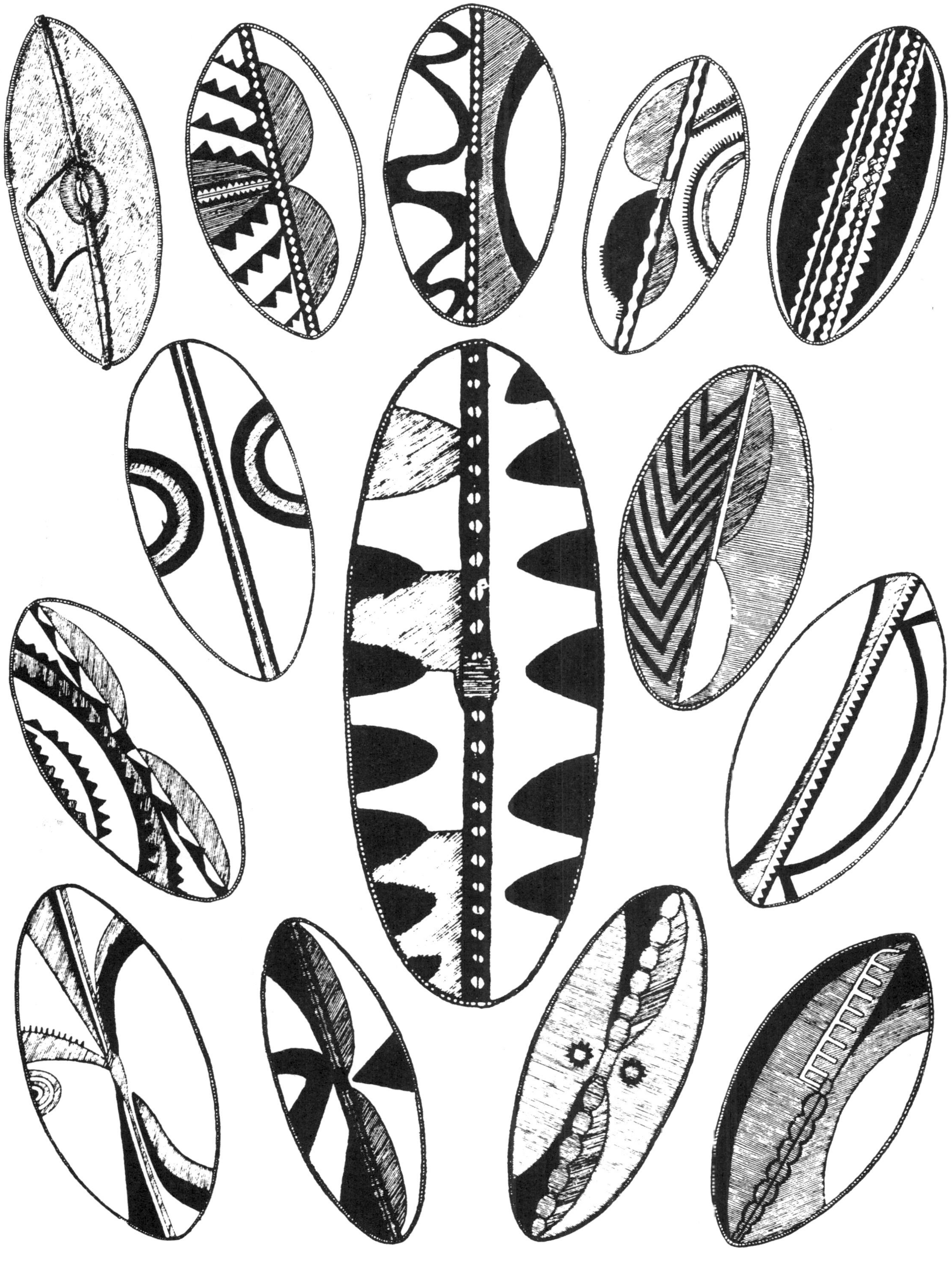

MUSESE TEXTILE DESIGN

Musese pile fabrics are crafted by the Kuba people of Zaire (formerly the Belgian Congo). Geometric designs are embroidered onto a woven raffia base cloth. To create the pile, the embroidered loops are left long, and then cut on one side of the cloth. Such fabrics were used ceremonially, as clothing, blankets, chair and stool adornments for high-ranking members of the tribe. These examples are from the collections of the Royal Museum for Central Africa, Tervueren, Belgium.

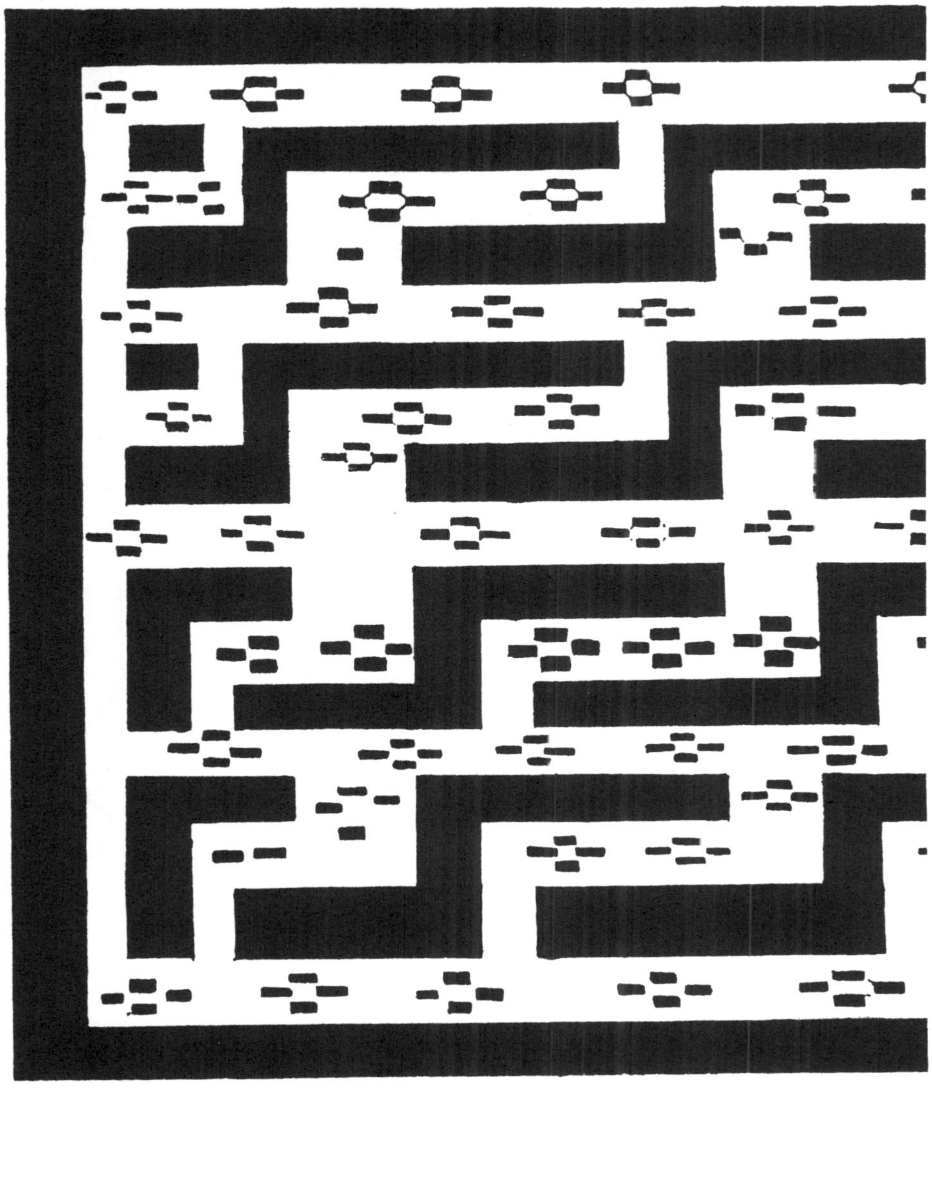

ANIMALS AND FIGURES

Above left and right wooden guardian figures from Guinea and Gabon; *above centre left* Bushman rock painting from S. W. Africa and *centre right* rock painting of fantastic creature from Rhodesia (now Zambia and Zimbabwe). *Opposite* images include a variety of lizard and snake designs; a mythical elephant *upper right* and a Ghanaian gold weight in the shape of a chameleon *lower right*.

ANIMAL MOTIFS

A selection of African animal motifs, including a scraped calabash stylized scorpion design from Dahomey *upper left,* and a wooden head-dress in the form of an antelope *above left.* Images *opposite* include a carved ivory feeding elephant *top left* from Nigeria; carved soapstone zebra and monkey designs from Zimbabwe *lower left and centre.*

MATS

Designs for flat-woven fibre mats from the Congo, showing schematized patterns of people, birds and a lizard.

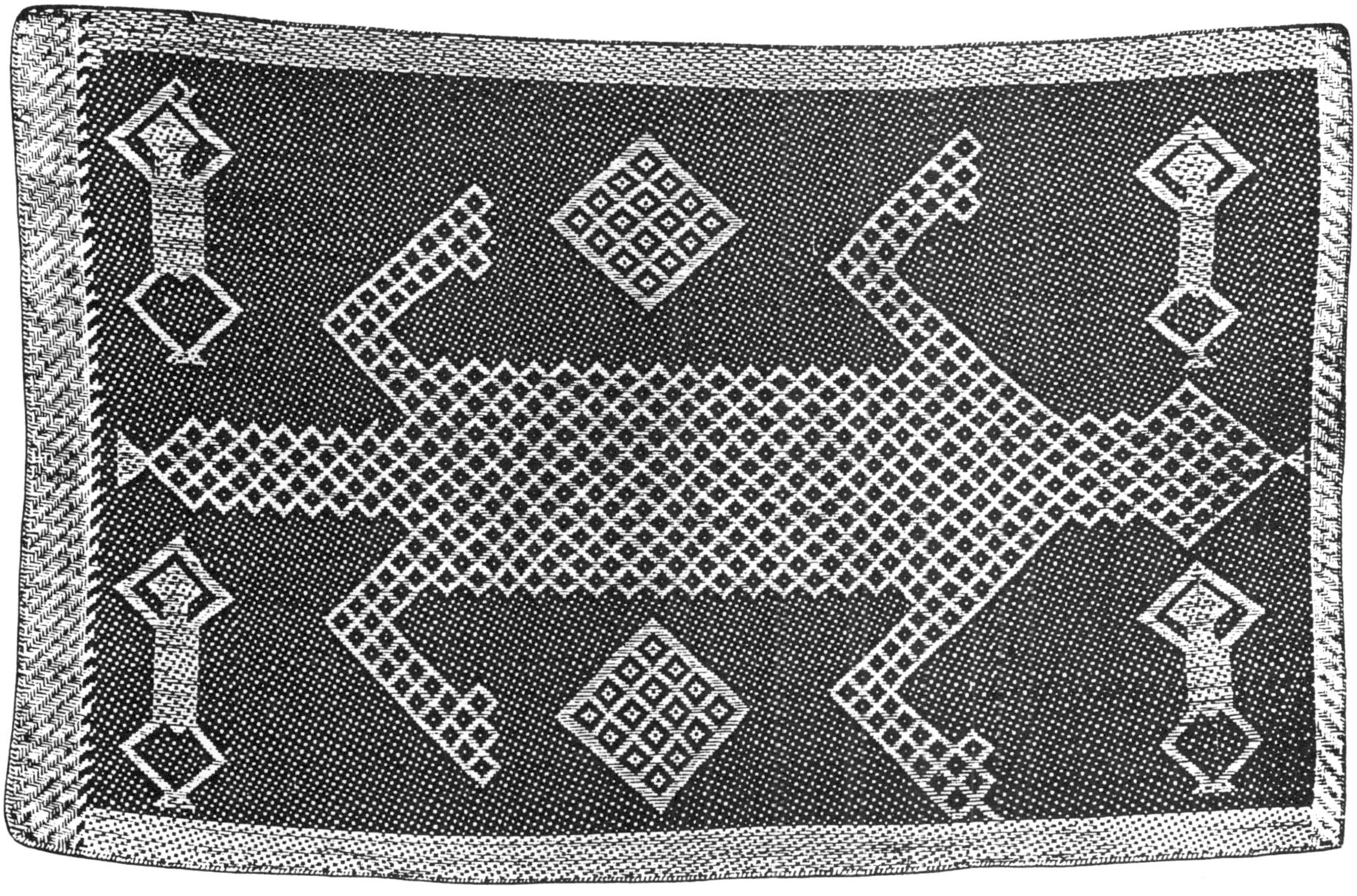

VESSELS FROM UKEREWE ISLAND, LAKE VICTORIA

The inhabitants of Ukerewe Island in Lake Victoria (also known as Lake Nyanza) made vessels out of wood and gourds, decorating them with simple but striking geometric patterns. *Top left and right and centre right* interior and side views of wooden dishes. *Centre left* milk container, *centre* bottle, *lower right* box made from bark and *lower right* drinking vessel made from a gourd.

THE AMERICAS

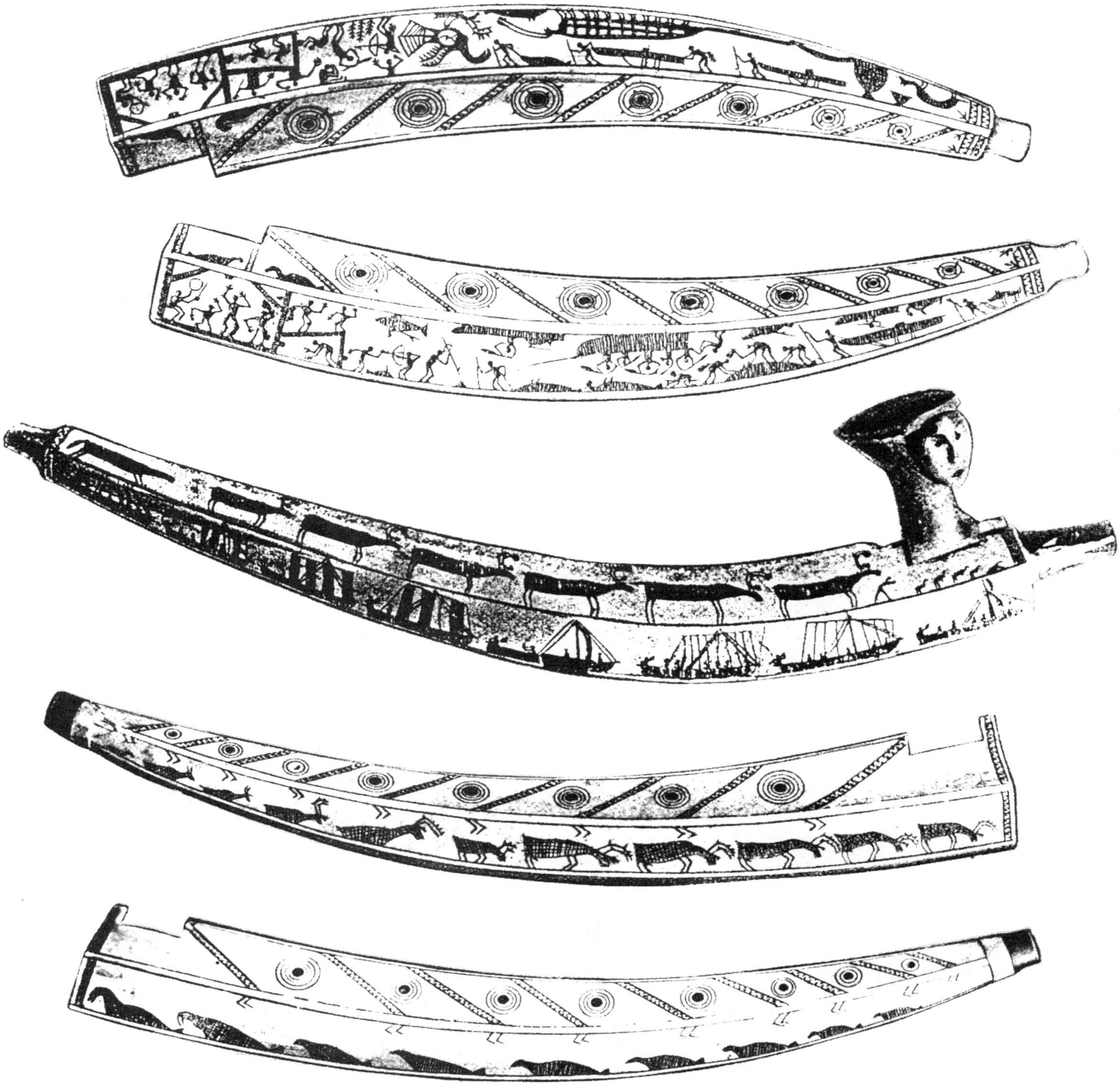

INUIT DESIGN

Walrus ivory pipe stems with incised pictographic decoration depicting scenes of Inuit daily life. The pairs *above and top* show the right and left sides of the same pipes. *Opposite top* are the obverse and reverse of a whale-line guide, placed on the bow of an umiak (sailing canoe), used in hunting, from Cape Prince of Wales. *Bottom* are ivory effigies: *l–r* an otter from Kushkunuk, a seal from Briston Bay, an otter from Minivak Island; *lower centre* is a seal from Kotzebue Sound, and *bottom* a walrus from Nashagak, Alaska.

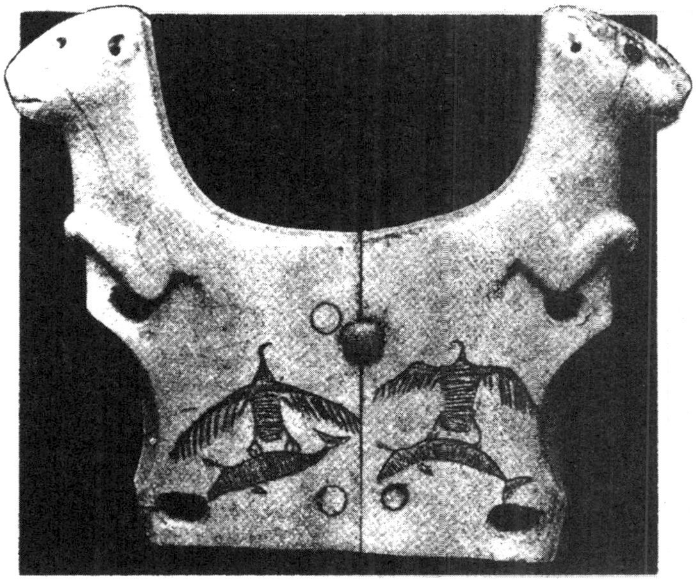

NORTH WEST AMERICAN NATIVE ART

Masks from British Columbia and Alberta, and *opposite* three totem poles from British Columbia. Carved and painted cedar or alder wood masks were used for ceremonial purposes in dances. The meaning of the two masks *top* is obscure: they may have been worn by dancers playing the roles of observers or gamblers in initiation ceremonies. The mask *above* is of a crooked beak type, and would have been worn on the forehead of a dancer, with a long fringe of cedar bark strips partially covering the head and body. Totem poles were placed outside the native wooden coastal houses; their accumulated stacks of carved images denote family crests, but other meanings are obscure.

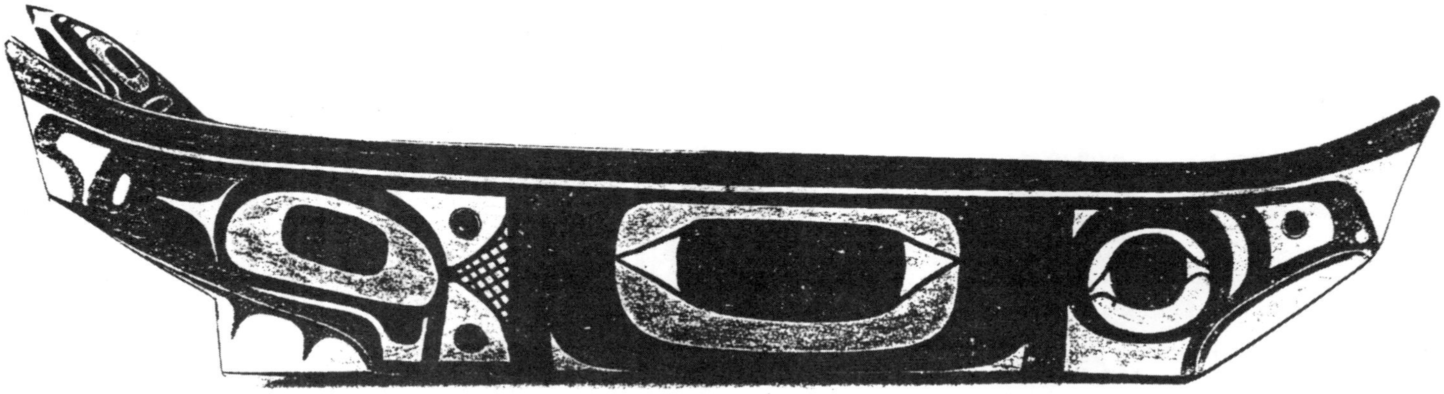

NORTH WEST COASTAL ART

Top and centre right are Alaskan wood carvings; *centre left* is an 18thC chief's basket in twined weaving, showing a whale hunt with harpoons from canoes, from Vancouver Island; *above* is a carved and painted model of a boat, possibly intended for use as a child's cradle. The images of the giant staring eye and bird's beak are typical. *Opposite* are ceremonial tools, including forks and ladles and *bottom right* a bailer.

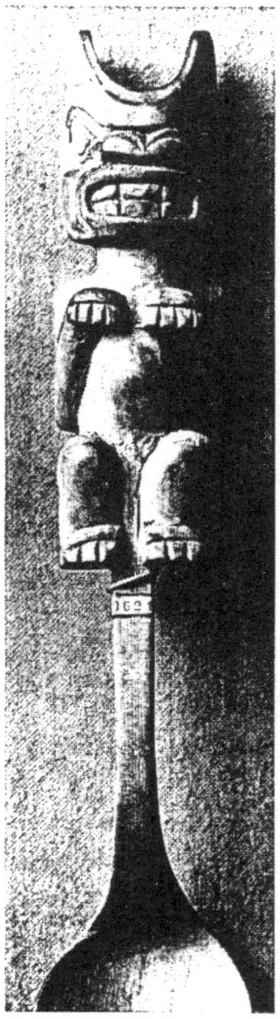

NORTH WEST COASTAL ART

Chilkat cloaks are hand-woven fringed blankets made of mountain goats' wool by the women of the Tsimshian and later Chilkat tribes: *top* is a painted design representing the Raven and perhaps two flat-fish on an 18thC Nootkan semi-circular cloak of cedar bark and nettle fibre, *opposite top* a Chilkat cloak hand-woven by Mary Ebbets Hunt (1823-1919), Fort Rupert, British Columbia, a member of the Tongas tribe of the Tlingit. *Above* is a woodcarving in the form of a dugout canoe, and *opposite* carved wooden pipes, all from Alaska.

NORTH AMERICAN DECORATIVE ARTS

This page shows 18thC decorative quillwork boxes from different provinces of Canada. *Opposite* are embroidered tobacco pouches and a mocassin, examples of Native American crafts from the Great Lakes strongly influenced in their designs by European folk embroideries.

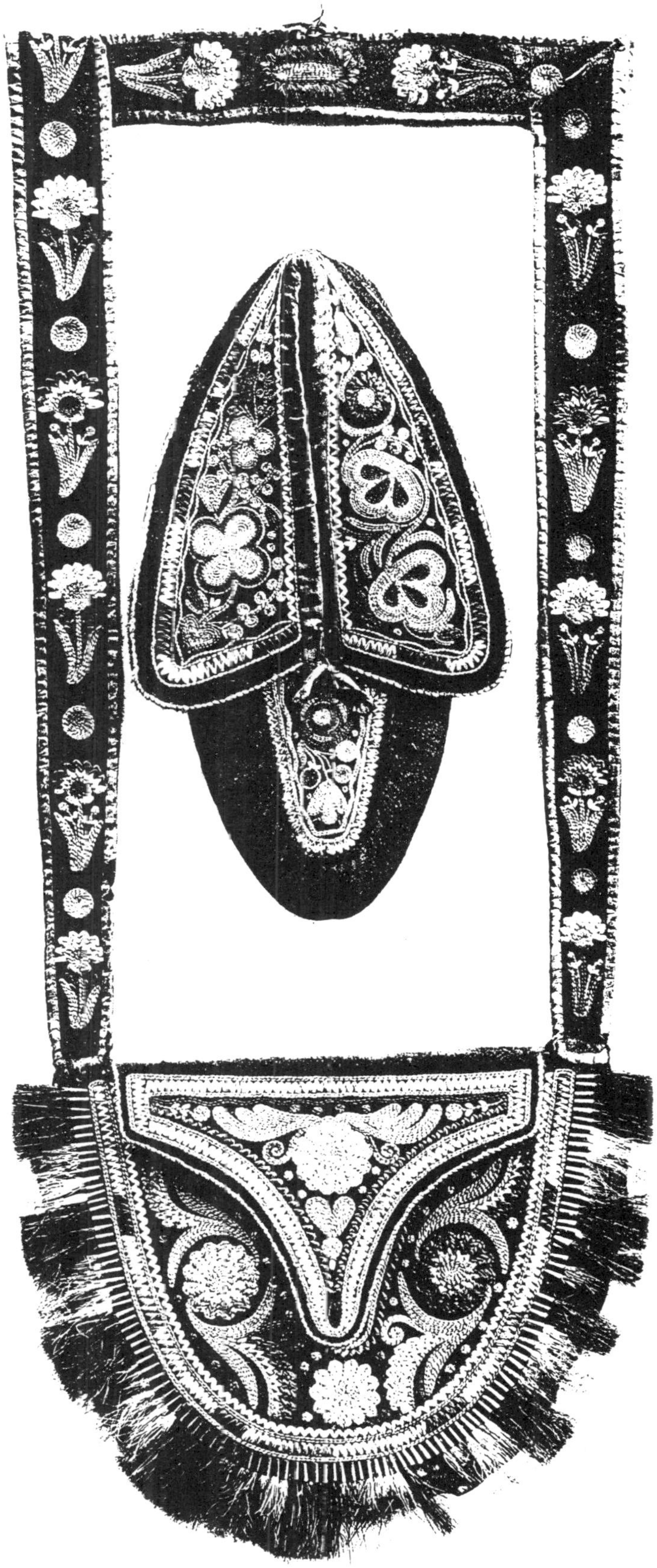

NATIVE AMERICAN ART

This page San Ildefonso designs recorded at the Indian Fairs, Santa Fe, in 1922 and 1923, and from items in the State Museum, Santa Fe. *Opposite* are border patterns from bead work: modern Hopi design, Indian School, Santa Fe; Santo Domingo; Tesuque; Casa Grandes; Modern Pueblo design, a variation of an old Zuni pattern; *bottom two rows* show prehistoric pottery designs.

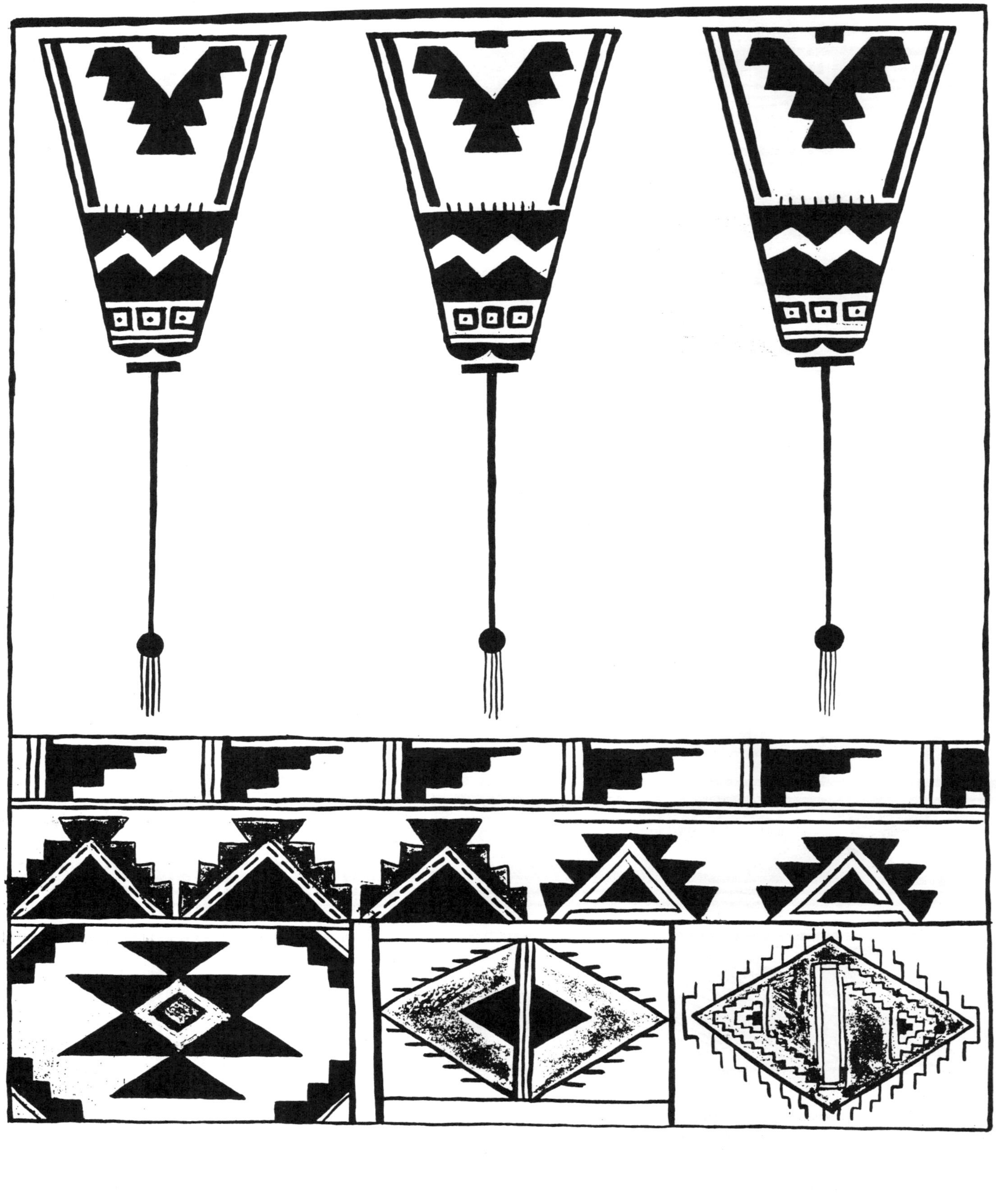

NATIVE AMERICAN ART

Border and frieze patterns and *opposite* ceramics and border patterns, from examples seen at the Indian Fair, Santa Fe, New Mexico, in 1922 and 1923, and in the State Museum, Santa Fe.

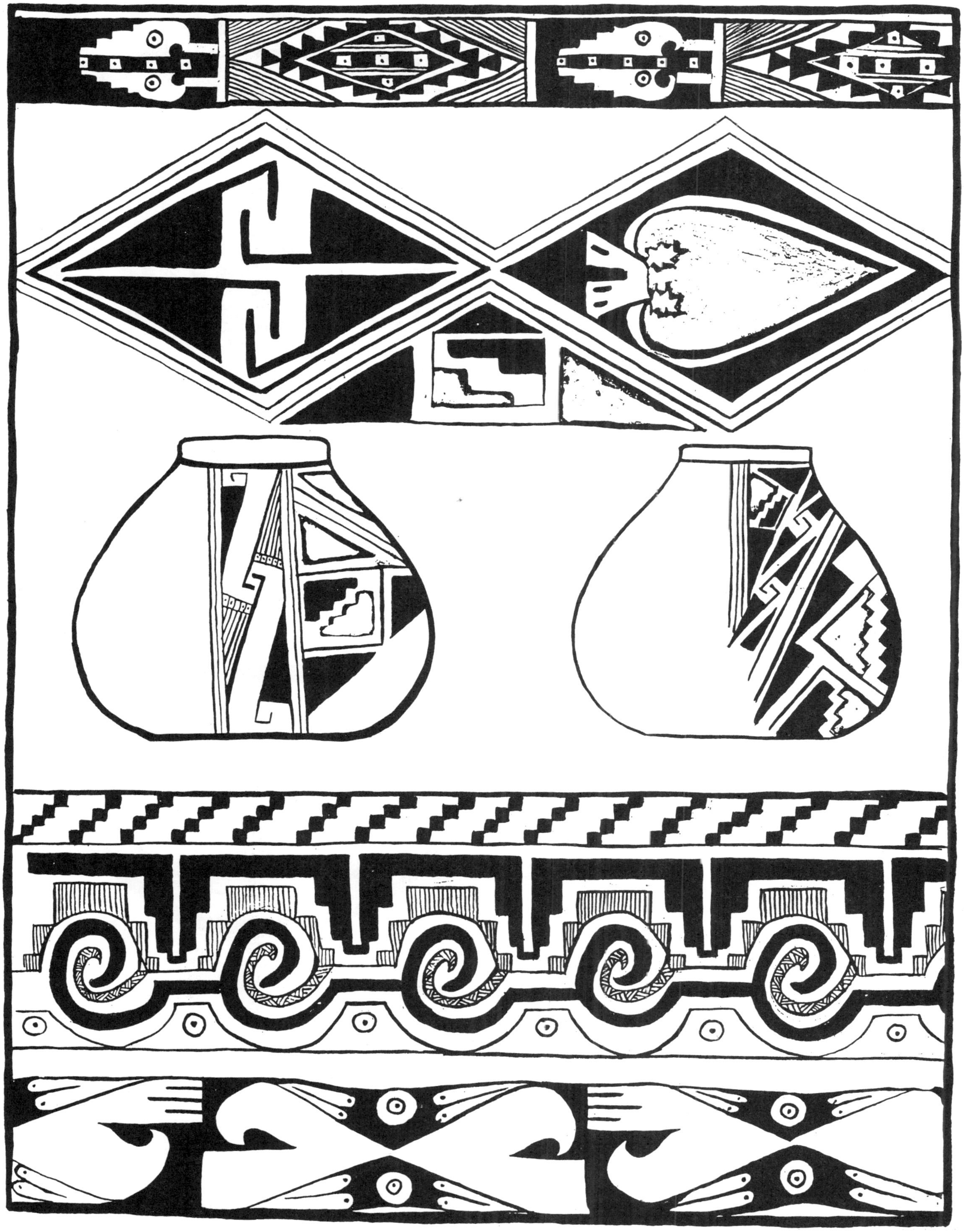

MOTIFS FROM NATIVE AMERICAN FOOD BOWLS

A collection of motifs from Arizona, now in the Smithsonian Institution, Washington, D.C. Images represent *top left* symbolic bird from Cunopavi; *top right* mythic bird from Chevlon; *centre left* plumed snake from Cunopavi; *above right* bird design from Homolobi. *Opposite top left* is a man-eagle; *top right* geometrical designs from Chaves Pass; *centre right* mythic birds and rain clouds symbols from Chevlon; *bottom left* plan view of a vase with bird decorations; and *bottom right* three lines of life from Chevlon.

AZTEC AND TOLTEC CERAMICS

Top and left are views of a funeral vase and its cover, found at St Jago Tlaltelolco, Mexico City. The mask represents the angel of death; the garland *below,* with alternate heads of corn and sunflowers, denotes the fullness of years. *Above and right* are examples of Toltec pottery.

AZTEC COSMOGRAPHY

An Aztec basalt calendar stone from Mexico City, made in 1479, in honour of the sun. The stone was made in the reign of King Axayacatl, in the year 13 acatl, and was originally placed horizontally in the grand temple of Mexico, in the part called Quauhaeilco. The complex imagery of the stone represents the different astronomical and cosmographical phases of the sun. The face in the centre represents the sun god throwing his light over the earth, symbolized by the tongue projecting from his lips. The hieroglyphics on the diadem encircling the head represent the division of time and the Mexican method of numbering the years.

TOLTEC CULTURE

Top left and right are images of Quetzalcoatl, god of air and wisdom, under his best-known attributes; he appears most often as the 'feathered serpent'. *Above* are three huge bas-reliefs from the palace at Palenque. *Opposite* are terra-cotta masks and heads found at Teotihuacan, the city of Quetzalcoatl and the place in which the universe was created; and *left and right* idols at Copan, where in 750, Mayan astronomers worked out the eclipses of the sun and the moon.

MAYAN SCULPTURES FROM PALENQUE

Near Palenque in south west Mexico lie the ruins of a major Mayan ceremonial centre, housing a remarkable series of relief sculptures in stone and in stucco which were recorded in a series of early 19thC engravings, from which this selection is taken.

MAYAN ART

Top left a god from an ancient Mayan manuscript; *top right* hieroglyphs representing the months in the Mayan calendar; *below right* the Peruvian jaguar god. *Above right and opposite* are details from a Mayan manuscript.

MEXICAN CERAMICS

Slip-decorated Mexican ceramics from Pueblos, now in the Ethnographical collections of the Trocadero, Paris. *Left and opposite top* are different sides of the same ewer. Techniques used include sgraffito (incised slip) *above right,* and painted brushwork. The example *opposite right* is earlier in date than the others, as shown by the schematic treatment of the birds and the 'slanted domino' border.

WOVEN TEXTILES

Warp-patterned handwoven sashes woven on back-strap looms from Mexico, Chile and Bolivia. Textiles were often used as barter currency. The various patterns shown were individual to their specific villages of origin, in a manner rather akin to the clan identities of Scottish tartans.

MEXICAN WOVEN DESIGNS

Intricately patterned bags and a belt double-woven on a backstrap loom by Huichol Indian weavers, Mexico, now in the ethnographical collections of the Trocadero, Paris.

MEXICAN POTTERY BORDERS

Border patterns from Mexican pottery in the collection of the British Museum, London.

MEXICAN ANIMAL MOTIFS

Decorative painted zoological motifs from Mexico, including an eagle *right,* and a dog *opposite top left,* from Colima, Cuautitlan, Guerrero, Huastec, Veracruz and Zempoala.

WOOD CARVING FROM VENEZUELA AND GUYANA

Combs, blades and clubs from Venezuela and Guyana.

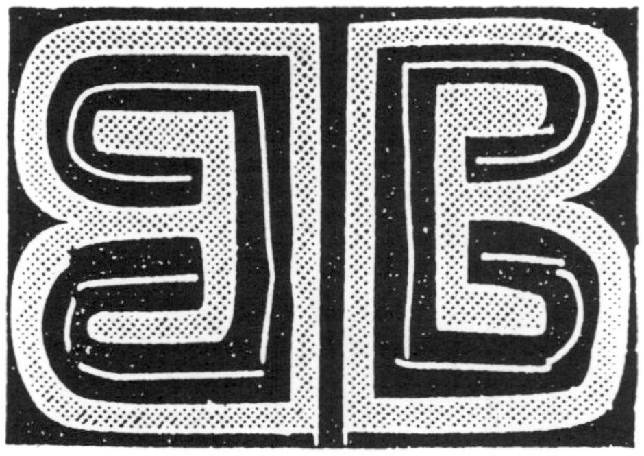

AMAZONIAN WOOD CARVING

Designs for wood carving from the native tribes of the Amazonian rain forest.

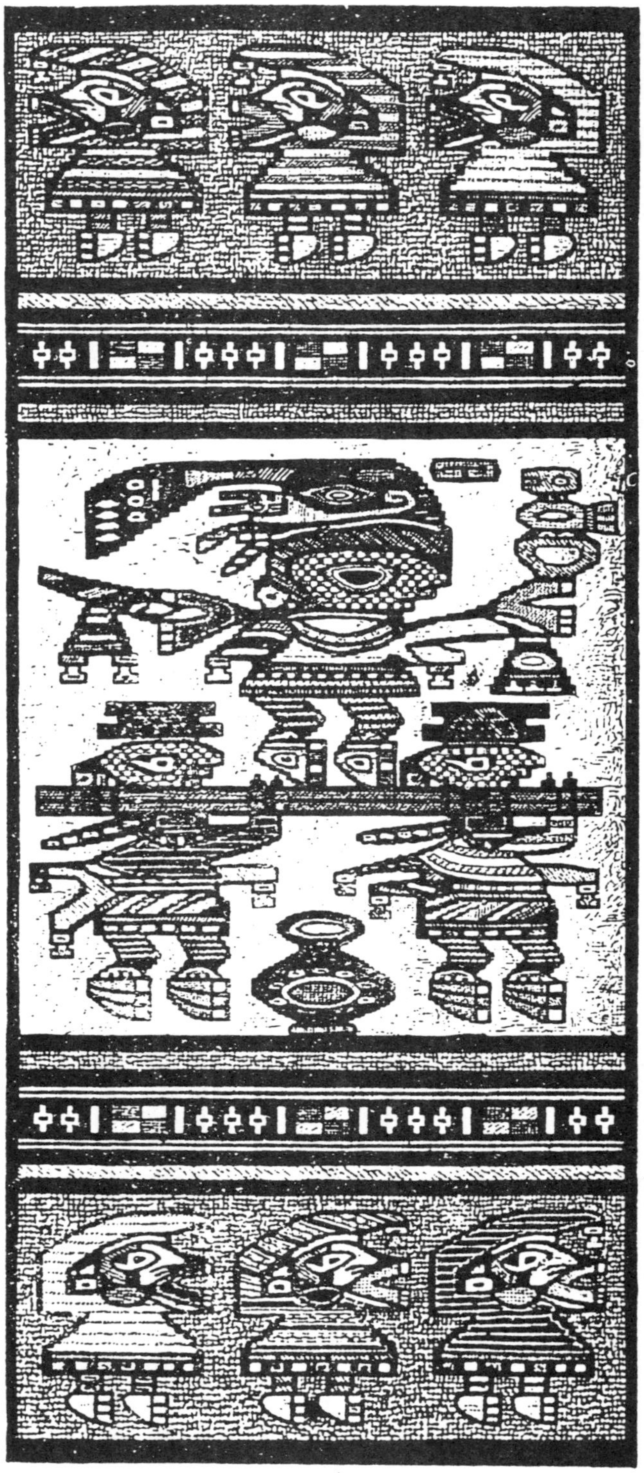

TEXTILES FROM GUYANA AND PERU

Opposite are beaded loin cloths from Guyana; *above left* is a woven hanging, possibly for a curtain, found at Ancon, Peru; *above right* is the central panel of a shroud, probably originally used as a curtain, found in the north Huaca (a pyramid made out of adobe bricks) at Gran Chimu, not far from the main palaces.

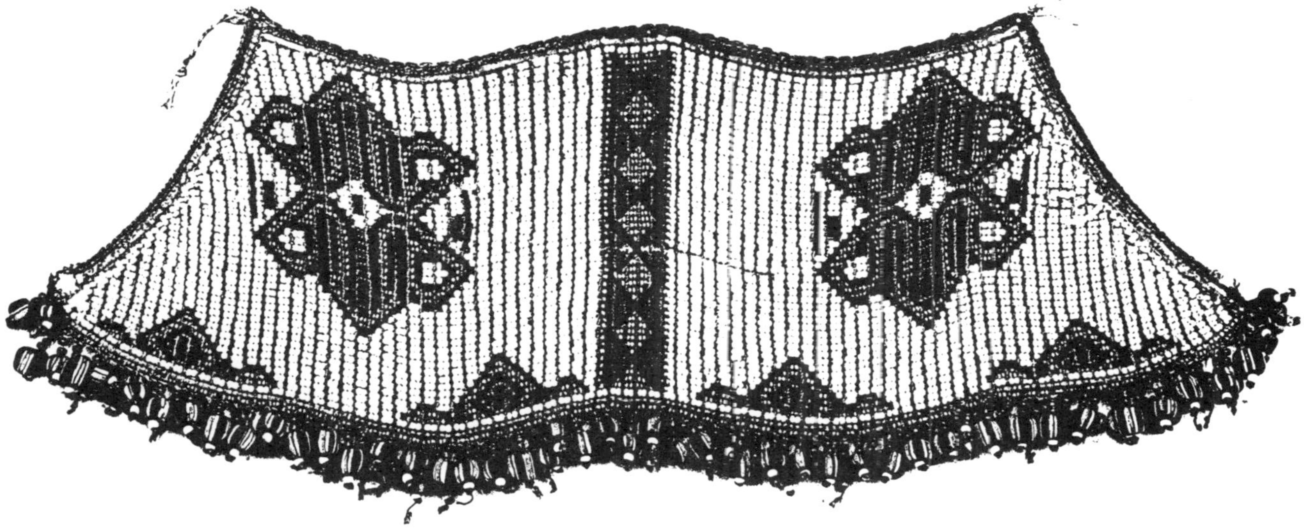

PERUVIAN CERAMICS

Coil-built Peruvian ceramic lamps and ewers are often zoomorphic in character. Designs such as the twin-spouted lidded cup *opposite second row, second from left* inspired the Victorian English designer Dr Christopher Dresser, who turned to South American ceramics as models for his pottery designs for the English Linthorpe pottery from Middlesbrough, Teeside.

PERUVIAN CERAMIC VESSELS AND METAL WHISTLES

Coil-built ceramic dishes, vases, jugs and a cup from a variety of different Peruvian sites, including Ancon, Quenco, Gran-chimu, Infantas, Cuzco and Moche; and *opposite* whistles in the forms of Peruvian birds and a cat, from Ancon, Chancay, Ollantaitambo and Paramonga.

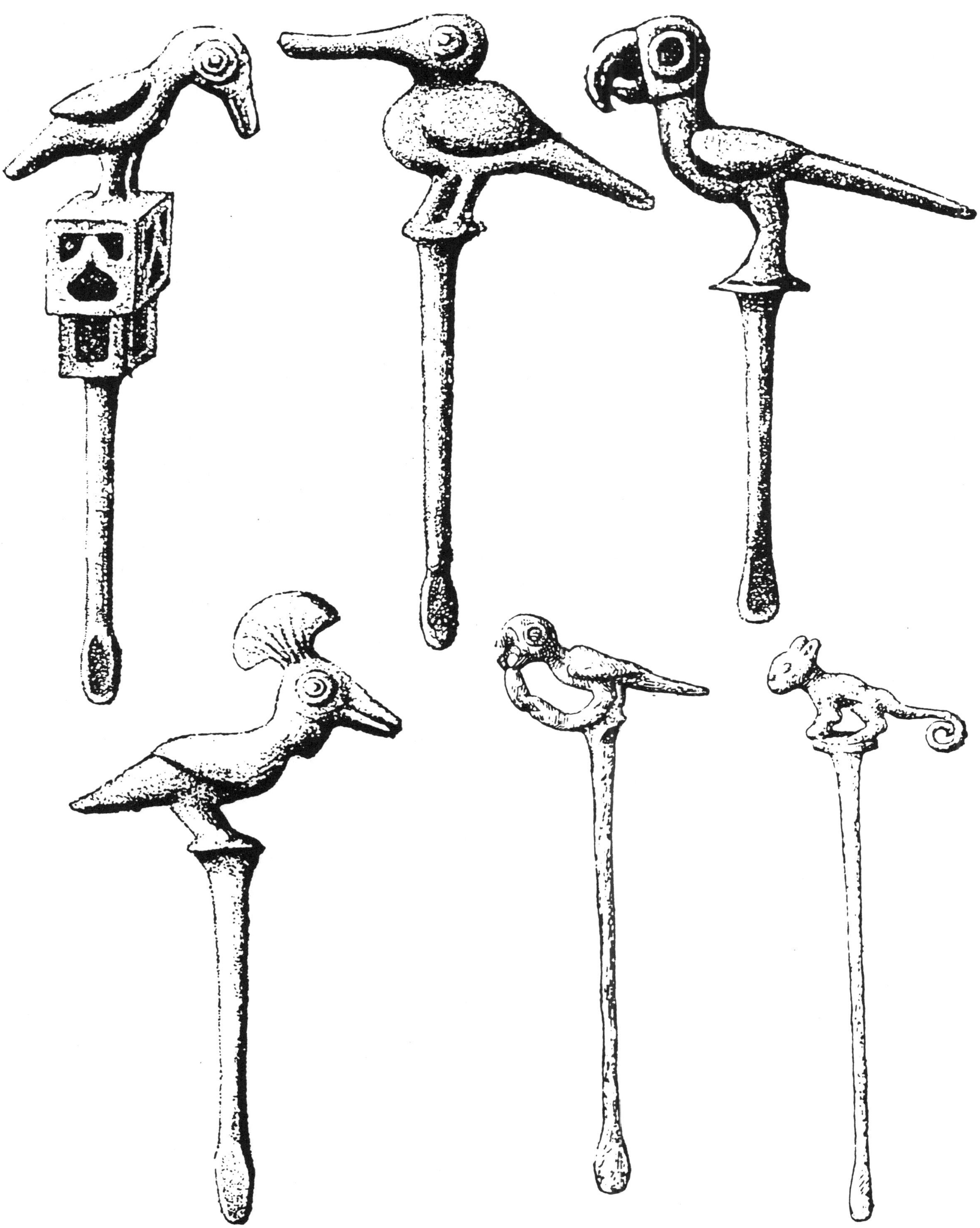

PERUVIAN TEXTILES

A selection of warp-faced handwoven Peruvian textile designs showing their predominantly geometric character; examples are from Ancon, Pachacamac, Moche, Paramonga and Chimbote.

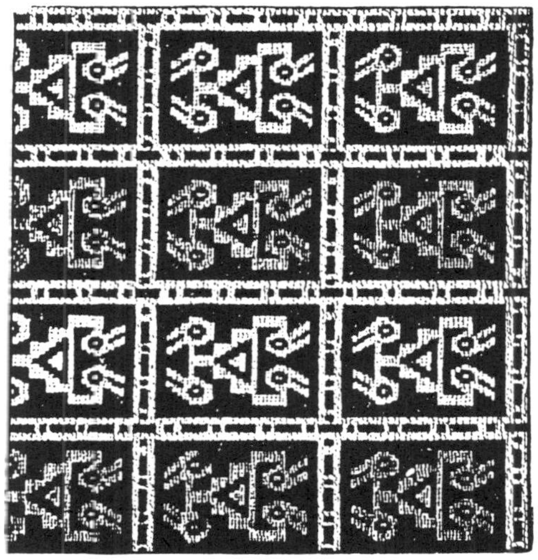

BOLIVIAN GODS

Right central bas-relief representing the Sun as Creator from the lintel of a monolithic doorway of the Sun at Tiahuanaco. The puma heads on the crown show the idol as lord over the strongest and fiercest animals. The head of the sceptre is of a condor (bird of prey) representing swiftness and power. *Left top and bottom* two figures of deities from the same lintel, flanking the central panel. *Left centre* bas-relief sculpture of the Sun from Pashash, now in the church at Cabana.

AUSTRALASIA

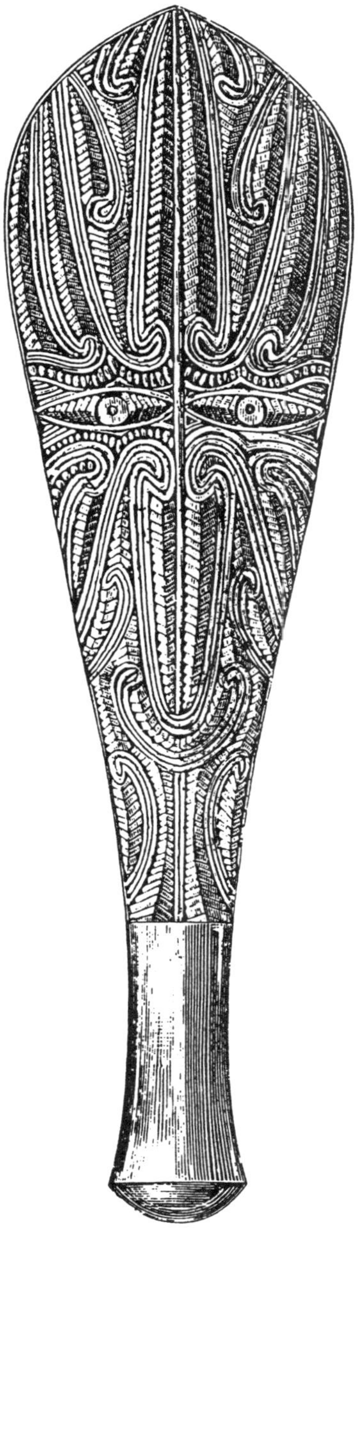

PAPUAN CARVINGS

The skulls of men killed in battle would be fixed to the top of the Papuan figure of an idol *top left. Top centre* is a Papuan wooden tablet with incised geometric ornamentation; *top right* a wooden shield shaped and painted in human form. *Above left and right* are hand-carved wooden heads of canoes from New Guinea.

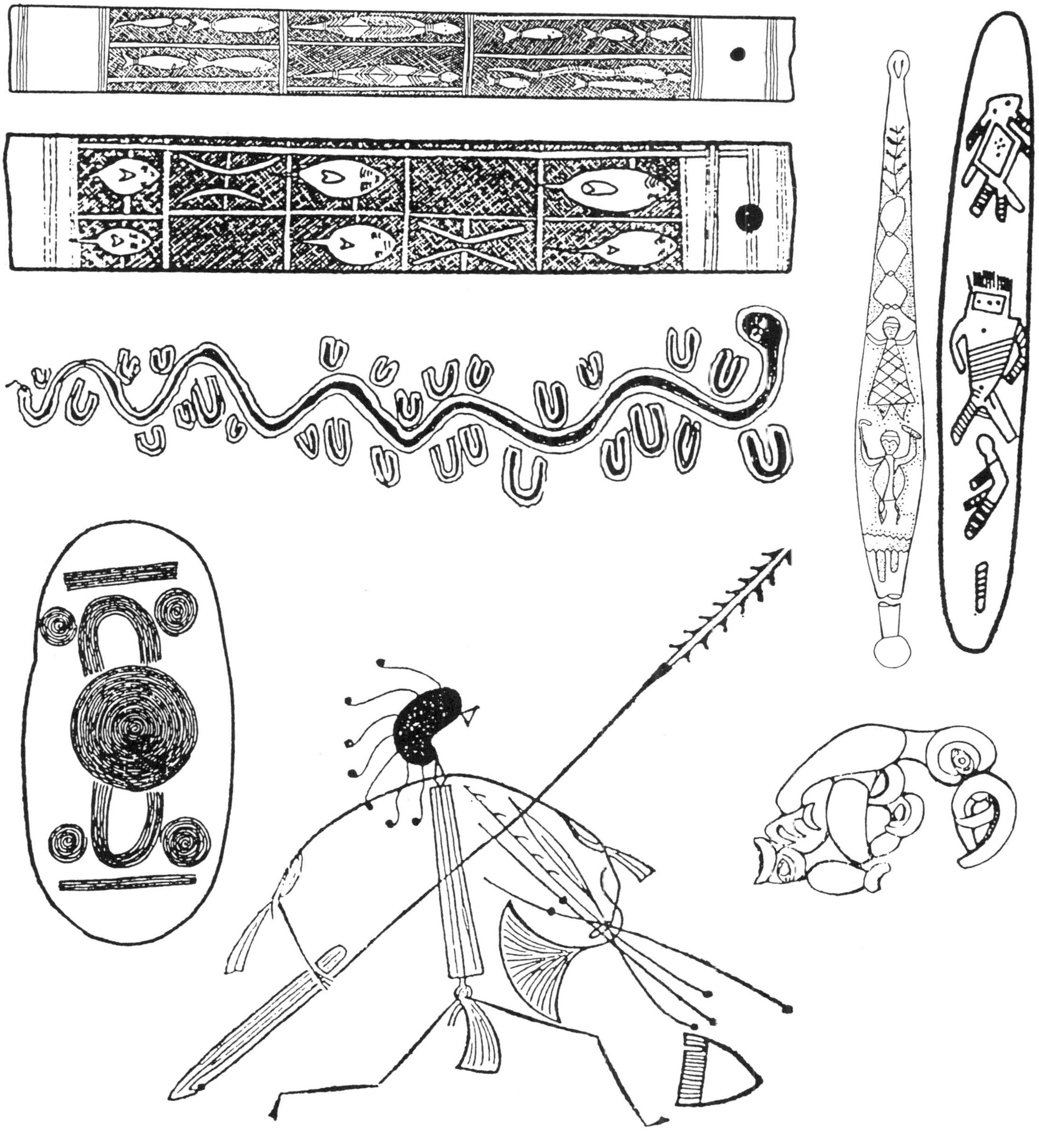

AUSTRALIAN ABORIGINAL IMAGERY

Top left are two carved smoking pipes from northern Australia; *below* these is a mythical snake surrounded by bands of wild dogs, from central Australia. *Top right* are objects carved with sacred motifs, from northern Australia. *Above left* is a woman's totem object; and *above centre* a warrior carrying a spear-thrower from Arnhem Land.

MAORI ART

Left is a mythical figure used as a common motif in New Zealand; *centre* is a Maori hand-carved ceremonial paddle, with profile and half-section details of handle shown *top right*.

MAORI ART

Right is a decorative carved image of a mythical figure from a Maori jewel box; *top left* is a Maori woodcarving of a female ancestor suckling her infant; *above left* is incised scroll work from a gourd bowl.

MAORI RAFTER PATTERNS

Examples of decoration applied to the rafters of Maori meeting houses, mostly from the east and north of the North Island, New Zealand. Maori traditions ascribe to Rauru, who lived in the Bay of Plenty area, the invention of the present pattern or style of Maori carving. The pigments used were mainly soot and red ochre, the white being the natural timber.

MAORI TATTOOING

Examples of the decorative patterns used in Maori skin tattooing. The pigment used was prepared by an elaborate ceremonial process involving the faeces from a Maori dog which had been made to consume a mixture of Kauri resin soot and bird fat. The dog's subsequent faeces were gathered, mixed and kneaded with birds' oil and water, left to dry, and then left buried in a container to cure before being used.

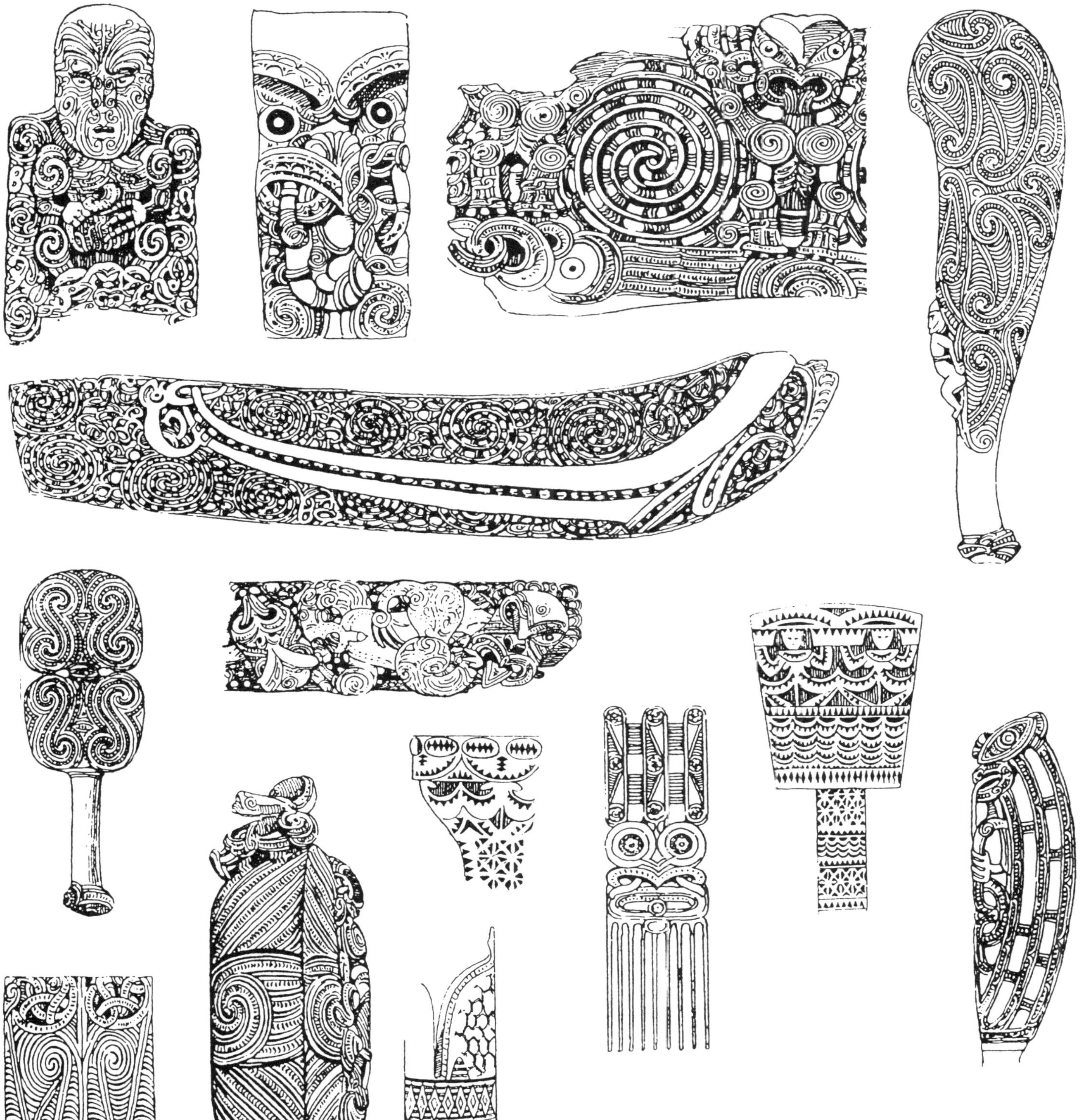

MAORI CARVING

Top row, l–r a human figure in carved wood; a Pataka slab (Auckland Museum); part of a carved lintel (Auckland Museum); a carved wooden club. Other items include the carved sternpost of a canoe *second row* (Auckland Museum); a carved wooden mere (ceremonial club) *third row, extreme left;* details from three carved and incised boxes; details of the heads of paddles; and a whalebone comb.

OCEANIC WOOD CARVING AND INCISED DECORATION

Ceremonial hand-carved wooden clubs and tools from Oceania, including examples from Tahiti, Hawaii, Fiji, New Zealand and the Tuamotu Archipelago. Images *opposite* include silhouettes engraved on a Fijian war club *top left and bottom right;* a plaited straw design from Hawaii *bottom left;* and *centre* a relief carving on a wooden bowl from the Marquesas islands.

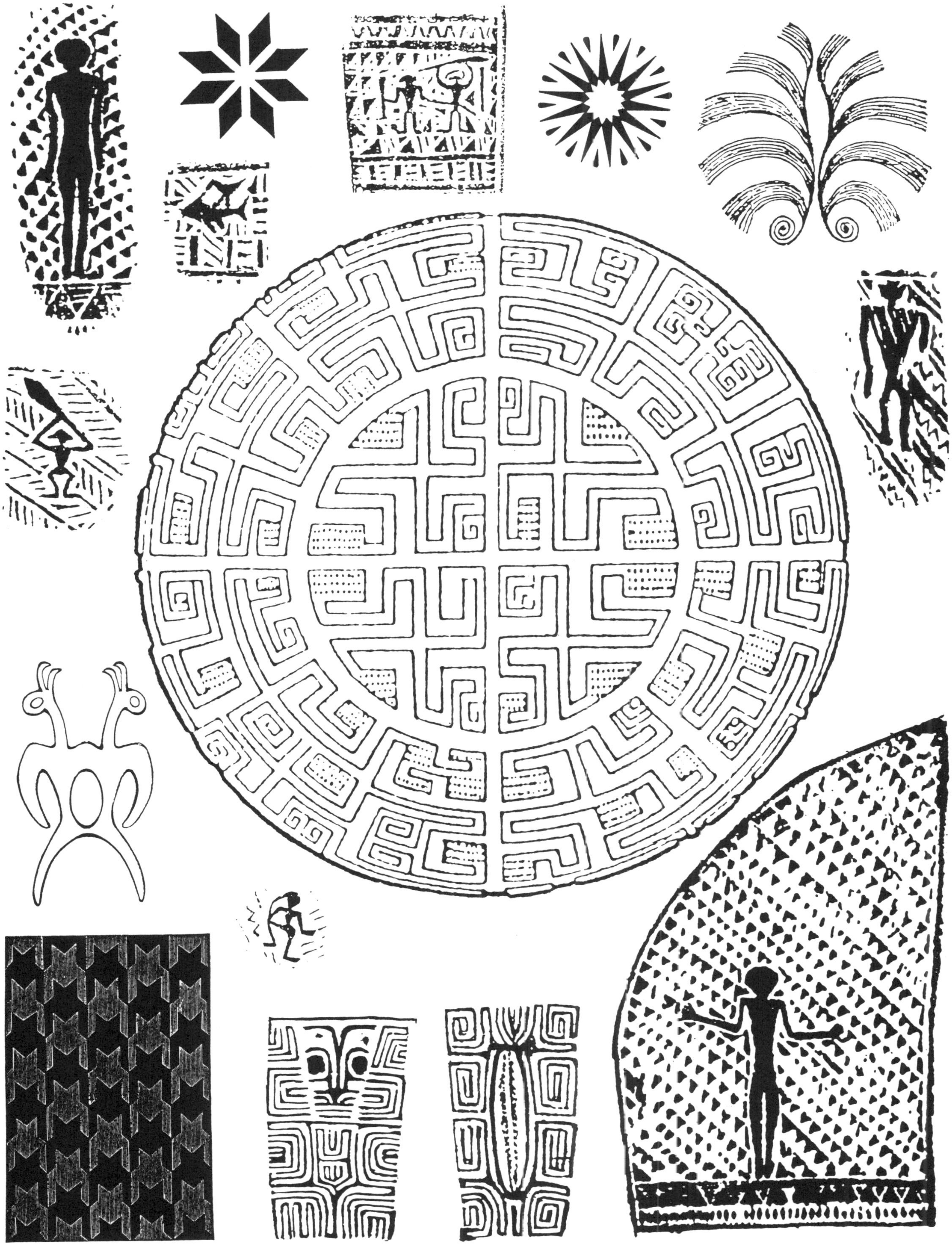

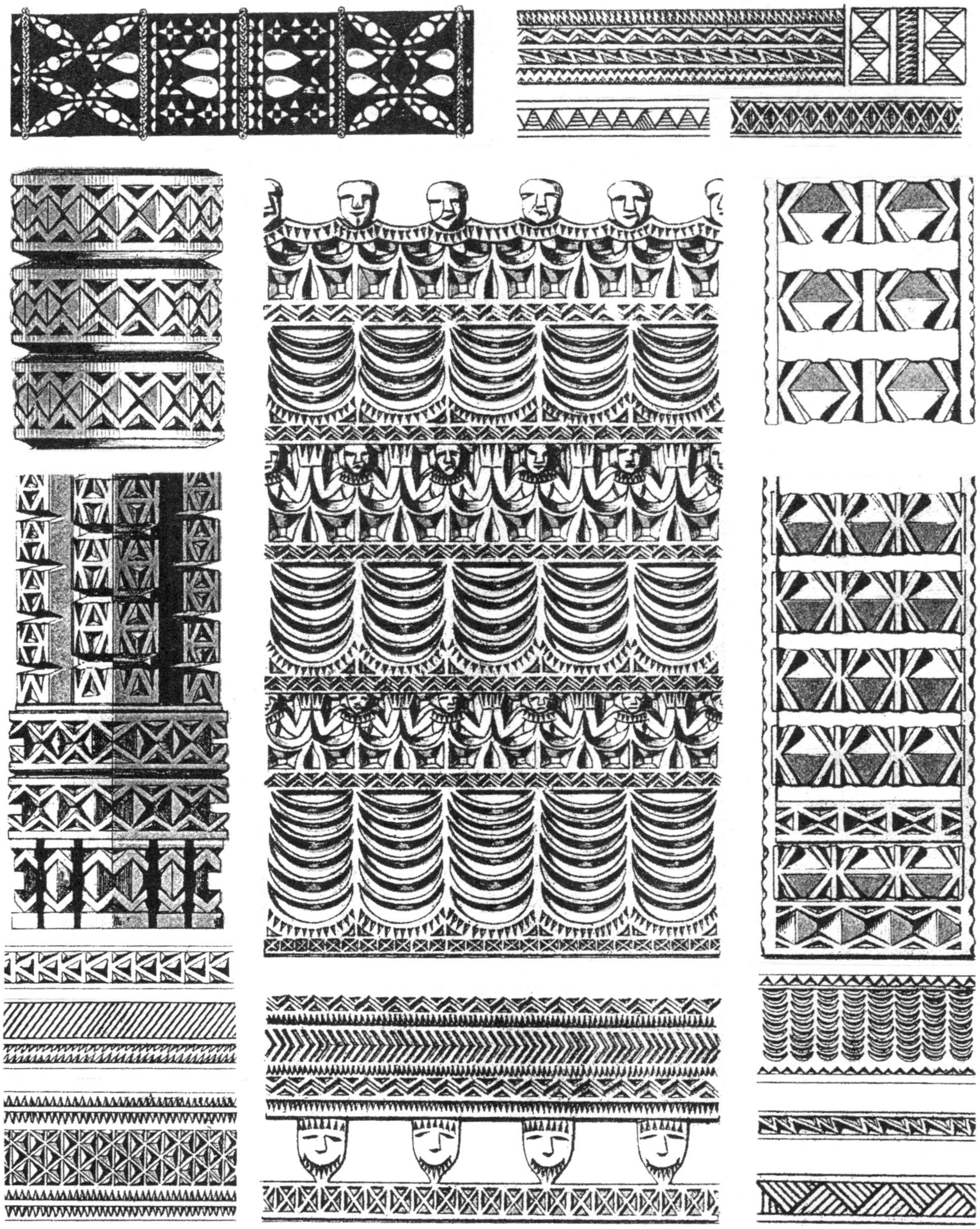

OCEANIC SURFACE DESIGN: TEXTILES AND LOW RELIEF CARVING

Above are examples of woven and block-printed textiles, made by hand from hibiscus bark and from paper mulberry, from Tonga, Otahiti, Hawaii and Fiji. *Opposite* are examples of carved low-relief decoration from Hawaii, the New Hebrides, Tonga and Tahiti, all from wooden tools and ceremonial weapons.

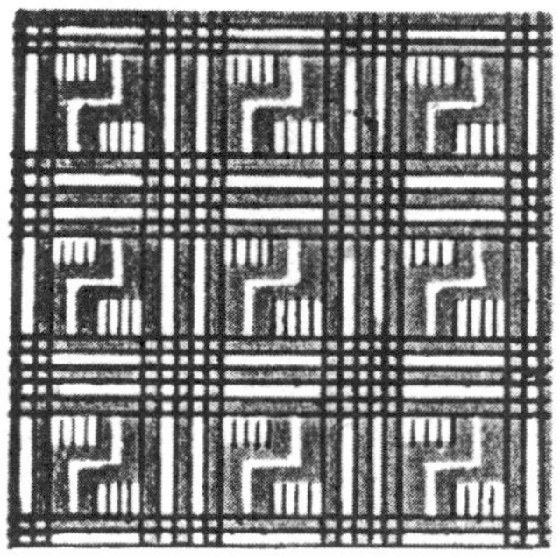

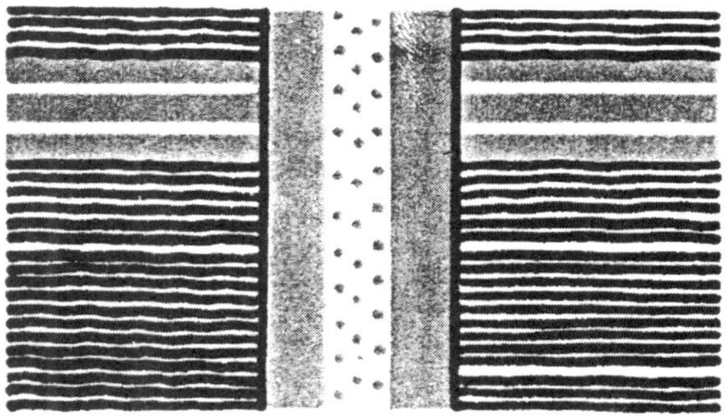

BIBLIOGRAPHY

ANNALES DU MUSEE DU CONGO BELGE, Tervueren, Ethnographie et Anthropologie (série III). *Notes analytiques sur les collections ethnographiques du Congo Belge. Tome II. Les industries indigiènes. Fasicule 2 et Dernier. Les nattes.* December, 1927.

ANSCOMBE, I. and GERE, C., *Arts and Crafts in Britain and America,* Academy Editions, 1978.

AUDSLEY, G. A. and CUTLER, T., *The Grammar of Japanese Ornament,* with an introduction by C. Newton, Studio Editions, 1989.

BABELON, E., *Manual of Oriental Antiquities,* H. Grevel and Co., 1889.

BEAUCLAIR, R., *Art Nouveau Patterns and Designs,* with an introduction by L. Suffield, Bracken Books, 1988.

BOWATER, M., *The Decorative Art of Russia,* originally published as *Slavonic and Eastern Ornamentation,* 1887. Re-published by Studio Editions Ltd, 1990.

BROCKLEHURST, T. U., *Mexico Today,* John Murray, 1883.

BRONSTED, J., *Early English Ornament,* Hachette Ltd, 1924.

CHANDA, J., *African Arts and Cultures,* Davis Publications Inc., Worcester, Mass., 1993.

CHARNAY, D., *The Ancient Cities of the New World,* Chapman and Hall, 1887.

COE, M. D., *The Maya,* Penguin Books Ltd, 1971, reprinted 1980.

COTTRELL, L., *The Penguin Book of Lost Worlds* (two volumes), Penguin Books Ltd, 1966.

COULSON, A. J., *A Bibliography of Design in Britain 1851– 1970,* Design Council, 1979.

D'AVENNES, P., *The Decorative Art of Arabia,* with an introduction by C. Newton, Studio Editions Ltd, 1989.

DEL RIO, CAPTAIN DON A., *Description of the ruins of an ancient city, discovered near Palenque in the kingdom of Guatemala in Spanish America,* including *Teatro Critico Americano,* by Dr P. F. Cabrera, Henry Berthoud, 1822.

DOBLHOFER, E., *Voices in Stone,* Paladin Books, Granada Publishing Ltd, 1973, reprinted 1979.

DRESSER, C., *Principles of Decorative Design,* Cassell, Petter and Galpin, 1873.

DRESSER, C., *Studies in Design,* originally published by Cassell, Petter and Galpin, 1876. Re-published by Studio Editions Ltd, 1988.

DRESSER, C., *The Art of Decorative Design,* Day and Son, 1862.

FEEST, C. F., *Native Arts of North America,* Thames and Hudson Ltd, 1980.

FEWKES, J. W., 'Preliminary account of an expedition to the Pueblo ruins in Winslow, Arizona', *Annual Report of the Board of Regents of the Smithsonian Institution, to July, 1896,* Government Printing Office, Washington, 1898.

FEWKES, J. W., 'Preliminary account of an expedition to the villages of the Red Rock Country, and the Tusayan ruins of Siyatki and Awatobi, Arizona, in 1895', *Annual Report of the Board of Regents of the Smithsonian Institution, to July 1895,* Government Printing Office, Washington, 1896.

FLEMING, J., HONOUR, H. and PEVNSER, N., *The Penguin Dictionary of Architecture,* Penguin Books Ltd, 2nd ed. 1972, reprinted 1977.

FROBENIUS, L., *Die Masken und Geheimbünde Afrikas,* Nova Akta abh. der Kaiserl. Leop.-Carol, Deutsche Akademie der Naturforscher, Band LXXIV., Nr. 1, Halle, 1898.

GILLON, W., *A Short History of African Art,* Penguin Books Ltd, 1986, reprinted 1991.

GLAZIER, R., *A Manual of Historic Ornament,* B. T. Batsford Ltd, 6th ed. 1948.

HAMILTON, A., *The Art Workmanship of the Maori Race in New Zealand,* Fergusson & Mitchell for the New Zealand Institute, Dunedin, 1896.

HARRIS, J. (ed.), *5000 Years of Textiles,* British Museum Press in association with the Whitworth Art Gallery and the Victoria & Albert Museum, 1993.

HASSELT, A. L. VAN, *Ethnographische Atlas van Midden-Sumatra met Verklarenden Tekst,* E. J. Brill, Leiden, 1881.

HAWTHORN, A., *Kwakiutl Art,* University of Washington Press, Seattle and London, 1979.

HOFFMANN, W. J., 'The Graphic Art of the Eskimos', *Annual Report of the Board of Regents of the Smithsonian Institution, for the year ending June 30 1895,* Report of the US National Museum, Government Printing Office, Washington, 1897.

HOLME, C. (ed.), *The Art-Revival in Austria,* The Studio, 1906.

HOUSTON, M. G., *Ancient Greek, Roman and Byzantine Costume and Decoration (including Cretan costume),* A. & C. Black Ltd, 1931.

INWARDS, R., *The Temple of the Andes,* privately printed by Vincent Brooks, Day and Son, 1884.

JENNESS, D., *Indians of Canada,* University of Toronto Press in association with the National Museum of Man, National Museums of Canada and Publishing Centre, Supply and Services, Ottowa, 7th ed. 1977, 5th reprint 1989.

JERVIS, S., *The Penguin Dictionary of Design and Designers*, Penguin Books Ltd, 1984.

JONES, O., *The Grammar of Chinese Ornament,* originally published by S. & T. Gilbert, 1867. Re-published by Studio Editions, 1987.

JONES, O., *The Grammar of Ornament,* originally published by Day and Son, 1856. Re-published by Studio Editions, 1986.

KOLLMANN, P., *The Victorian Nyanza,* Swan Sonnenschein & Co. Ltd, 1899.

LACROIX, P., *The Arts in the Middle Ages and at the Period of the Renaissance,* Chapman and Hall, 1870.

LAMBERT, D., *The Cambridge Guide to Prehistoric Man,* Cambridge University Press, 1987, reprinted 1989.

LEEDS, E. T., *Celtic Ornament in the British Isles down to AD 700,* Clarendon Press, 1933.

LEIGHTON, J., *Suggestions in Design, being a comprehensive series of original sketches in various styles of ornament arranged for application in the decorative and constructive arts,* Blackie & Son, 1880.

LOFTIE, W. J., *Lessons in the Art of Illuminating,* Blackie & Son, undated.

MAYER, B., *Mexico as it was and is,* J. Winchester, New York, with Wiley and Putnam, London and Paris, 1844.

McNEISH, J. and SIMMONS, D., *Art of the Pacific,* Oxford University Press in association with the Queen Elizabeth II Arts Council of New Zealand, 1979.

MEYER, F. S., *A Handbook of Ornament,* B. T. Batsford Ltd, 1894.

MOUNTFORD, C. P., *Aboriginal Paintings from Australia,* a Mentor-UNESCO Art Book, The New American Library of World Literature Inc., 1964.

PULSZKY, DR C. V., *Ornamente der Hausindustrie,* Ungarns, Budapest 1878, gedruckt in der Kön. Ung. Universitas Buchdruckerei.

RACINET, A., *The Dictionary of Ornament,* originally published as *Deuxième Série de l'Ornement Polychrome,* by Firmin-Didot et Cie, Paris, 1885. Re-published by Studio Editions Ltd, 1990.

RACINET, A., *The Encyclopedia of Ornament,* originally published as *Original Polychromatic Ornament* by Henry Sotheran & Co., 1873. Re-published by Studio Editions, 1988.

REAL, D., *La Décoration Primitive, Amérique post-Colombienne,* Librairie des Arts Décoratifs, Paris, 1924.

ROCKHILL, W. W., *The Land of the Lamas; notes of a journey through China, Mongolia and Tibet,* Longmans, Green & Co., 1891.

SPELTZ, A., *The Styles of Ornament, from prehistoric times to the middle of the XIVth century,* B. T. Batsford Ltd, 1910.

STRANGE, T. A., *A Guide to Collectors. 3,500 illustrations. English furniture, decoration, woodwork, allied arts during the last half of the seventeenth century, the whole of the eighteenth century, and the earlier part of the nineteenth,* Studio Editions Ltd, 1994.

STRONGE, S., *The Decorative Art of India,* Studio Editions Ltd, 1990.

STUDIO, THE, An illustrated magazine of fine and applied art, vols. 3, 4, 1894, and extra winter numbers for 1894, 1896, 1897 and 1898.

TALBOT RICE, D., *Islamic Art,* Thames and Hudson Ltd, 1965, rev. ed. 1975, reprinted 1979.

WARING, J. B., *Illustrations of Architecture and Ornament,* Day and Son, 1865.

WIENER, C., *Pérou et Bolivie, récit de voyage suivi d'etudes archéologiques et éthnographiques de notes sur l'écriture et les langues des populations indiennes,* Librairie Hachette Ltd, 1880.

WILLETT, F., *African Art, an introduction,* Thames and Hudson Ltd, 1971.

WILSON, E., *8000 Years of Ornament, an illustrated handbook of motifs,* British Museum Press, 1994.

WILSON, E., *North American Indian Designs,* British Museum Pattern Books, A Colonnade Book, British Museum Publications, 1984.

WIRE, D. and LAING, J., *The Encyclopedia of Signs and Symbols,* Studio Editions Ltd, 1993.

WORNUM, R., *Analysis of Ornament, the Characteristics of Styles: an introduction to the study of the history of ornamental art,* Chapman and Hall, 1856.

ZELIZKO, J. V. and HOLUB, DR E., *Felsgravierungen der Südafrikanischen Buschmänner,* F. A. Brockhaus, Leipsig, 1925.